POINT-TO-POINTING

POINT-TO-POINTING

*A History
An Introduction
and
A Guide*

TERENCE BRADY and MICHAEL FELTON

PELHAM BOOKS

PELHAM BOOKS

Published by the Penguin Group
27 Wrights Lane, London W8 5TZ, England
Viking Penguin, a division of Penguin Books USA Inc, 375 Hudson Street, New York,
New York 10014, USA
Penguin Books Australia Ltd, Ringwood, Victoria, Australia
Penguin Books Canada Ltd, 2801 John Street, Markham, Ontario, Canada L3R 1B4
Penguin Books (NZ) Ltd, 182–190 Wairau Road, Auckland 10, New Zealand

Penguin Books Ltd, Registered Offices: Harmondsworth, Middlesex, England

First published 1991

Copyright © Terence Brady and Michael Felton 1991

Typeset in Linotron 10½ on 12½ Meridien by Cambrian Typesetters, Frimley
Printed and bound in Great Britain by Butler and Tanner Ltd., Frome

A CIP catalogue for this book is available from the British Library

ISBN 0 7207 1931 3

In a few instances it has not been possible to ascertain the copyright owner of the
illustrations and it is hoped that any omissions will be excused.

*Point-to-pointers have raced 'all-weather' long before Lingfield and
Southwell. The 1983 Men's Open at Cottenham, won aptly enough by
General Confusion (no 8).* (Mike Roberts)

CONTENTS

FOREWORD
BY JOHN OAKSEY

If only Terence Brady and Michael Felton had produced this book forty years ago the whole history of point-to-pointing – well, to be exact, the whole history of the VWH Members' and Bar Lightweight races – would have been entirely different. Because those were the prizes on which my father and I set our hearts in 1950 and with Brady and Felton to guide us I cannot believe that we would have been quite so unsuccessful. Even our solitary Pegasus Club triumph, to tell the truth, was only made possible by the refusal of the other seven runners at the Kimble Open Ditch!

How differently we would have set about it with Terence and Mike to guide us. For after three fascinating chapters about the early years – which confirm that the birth of pointing was also the birth of steeplechasing – there is no aspect of the game the authors overlook. Although not quite so outspoken as Messrs Mackenzie and Selby, they never shrink from controversial issues. The more arrogant and reactionary denizens of the hunting world are eloquently described and the theory that the end of foxhunting would mean the end of point-to-pointing is curtly and convincingly dismissed.

But by far the best and most valuable feature of this book is the sensible advice it contains. One chapter is called 'To do or not to do' – and, whether you want to buy a point-to-pointer, choose someone to train him, prepare yourself to ride him, run a meeting – or just go to enjoy yourself, you will find the best way to do it on these pages.

Perhaps, for a beginner in any of the various fields, the best advice of all is not to be afraid of *asking*. I agree wholeheartedly with the authors that the intensely competitive world of pointing is also a kind and helpful world, provided you are prepared to ask. But, besides asking, read and enjoy this book.

AUTHORS' FOREWORD

In order to stay healthy, a sport must regularly check-up on the soundness of its constitution. And as far as point-to-pointing is concerned, there is little doubt that in recent years those actively involved in the running of it have become increasingly aware of the need for continual surveillance, in order that the quality of the sport may be constantly improved. Even as we write, a Working Party appointed by the MFHA Point-to-Point Sub Committee has been set up to investigate what changes, if any, might be necessary in the framing of races, and to consider what the options might be. Suggestions have already been outlined, and at present are being considered by those involved in the sport, but to date no firm recommendations have been made. Even so, the diligence of the Sub Committee is an ample enough illustration of the concern being shown for the future of the sport by those who govern it.

On the other hand there are many diehards who will resist the suggestion of even more change, just as they resisted all previous up-dates, since they believe most sincerely that yet more improvements will only make what is after all intended to be an amateur sport yet more 'professional'. These points are examined in the text, but we only make mention of them here due to the fact that because the sport is under such constant scrutiny, by the time this is published some of what we say may already be out of date, and if any such solecisms appear, then we apologise.

For instance, there are various recommendations suggested for the season of 1991, such as a possible earlier starting date, due to the apparent change in our winter climate, the introduction of jockeys' medical cards, that Adjacent races need reframing and reforming, that the recently introduced 2½ mile 'novice' races should be confined to the early part of the season when the ground is usually softer and therefore more favourable for the running of young horses, and that walk-overs should not count towards the final tally in the championship contests, etc. There has also been a welcome move to allow those actively involved in the administration and the running of the sport to have more say at 'government' level, via the Point-to-Point Owners' Association, and its representation on the MFHA committee (see Appendix 1). At the moment of writing the PPOA's only member on the committee has no vote, which seems a little foolish, to say the least.

But if there are solecisms, if some of what we say by the time you read it is out of date, we also rejoice at the fact, because it means that the sport, by recommending and hopefully making constant changes, is in good heart, and long may it remain so.

We would also like to take this opportunity to thank all those who so willingly and cheerfully helped us collect and collate the information needed to compile a book of this nature, in particular Robert and Sally Alner, Nigel Bloom, Hugh Condry, Simon Claisse, Keith Cummings, Simon, Penelope and Tabitha Cave, John and Jane Dufosee, Peter Dufosee, Sandy Dudgeon, David Naylor-Leyland, Paul Hacking, *Horse and Hound*, Rupert Nuttall, Lord Oaksey, Tim Thomson Jones, John and Jackie Porter, Charles Stebbing, Terence Selby, Caroline Saunders, Philip Scofield, Charles Sample, Percy Tory, James Weatherby, Michael Williams, William Walters.

To all those named, and to the thousands unnamed, the enthusiasts who love to watch or to participate in this wonderful sport, we dedicate this book, as we do to those magnificent creatures without whom winter would just be a black hole, because without them there would be no such thing as racing between the flags – the horses.

T.B.
M.F.
1990

At the Start

*'The world is round and the place which may seem like the
end may also be only the beginning.'*

If history is to be believed, then the flag was dropped on the first
point-to-point races not as generally believed in the countryside
of Ireland or England but instead in America, in the streets of
Jamestown, Virginia, whither many of the Cavalier families from
England had fled from Cromwell after the Civil War. For
apparently one of the very first by-laws framed by Jamestown's
town council was to 'prohibit point-to-point racing in the
streets'. However, since it is highly unlikely that these urban
Virginian 'point-to-pointers' found anything of note over which
to jump in the town's thoroughfare this claim must be
considered specious, and credence should be given to the more
traditionally held belief that the sport was born in the British
Isles.

Exactly where conception took place is a point still readily
contended. Ireland makes the most strenuous claim, citing the
famous four and a half mile 'steeplechase' of 1752 which was
run between the churches of Buttevant and St Leger as the first
officially recorded instance of the sport, but since the race
involved only two horses, ridden by Messrs Blake and
O'Callaghan, and thus was not a steeplechase *per se* but rather a
'match', those opposing the Irish claim argue that such matches
had been held in England long before this date, the most notable
of them being the victory of the Lord Suffolk over the Duke of
Richmond as early as March 1662.

The Steeplechasing for England faction give as the sport's
starting date a time some forty years on from the Irish race, the
year 1790, or 1792, depending on which reference book you
choose to believe. This was, it is claimed, when the first 'proper'
steeplechase was run, proper because it involved more than two
participants, but only just. There were three contestants in the

race, Mr Charles Meynell, Sir Gilbert Heathcote, and Lord Forester, and they chased each other over eight Leicestershire miles, from Barkby Holt to Billesdon Coplow and back again, for a purse of 100 guineas a man. The contestants could choose their own line, and Mr Charles Meynell emerged the winner. The first recorded Irish steeplechase with more than two runners was not held until 1793 at Ballyshannon.

However, in defence of the Irish cause, and their claim to be the nursery of steeplechasing, it must be pointed out that if the number of contestants is discounted then cross-country jumping races had been going on for a lot longer and with much greater regularity in Ireland than they had in England. Throughout the 18th century and most probably in the latter part of the preceding one, the 'mad' Irish gentry had taken each other on in the sport of 'pounding'. This was an extremely dangerous version of 'follow-my-leader', since the route the two protagonists were to take was chosen by whichever of them won the toss. The winner of the draw also set the pace, leaving his opponent to 'chase' him or sometimes quite literally to die in the attempt, because victory was accorded only after one of the competitors had defaulted, or been 'pounded' to a standstill.

The start of the 1833 Northampton Grand Steeple Chase. Races were then being run in 'bee-lines'. This would have been the last sight these spectators would have had of the contestants. (Arthur Ackermann & Son Ltd)

The sport was finally accorded the title of 'steeplechasing' when it was eventually agreed to run these 'matches' over a set line of country, and since church spires were usually the most remarkable features in the chosen landscape, the competitors more often than not used them as their nominated finishing points. And herein lies the paradox at the heart of the history of the 'winter game'. For it is generally assumed that 'point-to-pointing' evolved from 'steeplechasing', whereas in fact the early 'steeplechases' were all quite literally point-to-points, because they were run in bee lines. And it was not until long after the sport of 'steeplechasing' had been established that races were ever run otherwise. Steeplechases raced circuitously as is the norm nowadays were mid-19th century refinements, while straight line point-to-points were occasionally still being run as late as the mid-1930s. So really rather than contending that point-to-pointing was an offshoot of steeplechasing, it would perhaps be more accurate to suppose that the opposite was true, and that point-to-pointing was indeed the father of the sport.

What there is absolutely no doubt about is that the sport of racing horses over obstacles was inspired by one thing alone, namely foxhunting. The fox had been hunted for centuries, but was considered not worthy of the chase, and so until the mid-18th century had simply been run to ground by hounds then dug out and killed unceremoniously. The stag, the hare, the wolf and the wild boar were the prize quarry, and were hunted with hounds on foot through the great forests which then covered Britain. Horses were only utilised where space allowed; that is, in forests where special rides had been cut, or in country such as the New Forest where large areas of open heath lay between the vast and dense woodlands.

So it was not until the forests had been greatly reduced in the early 18th century that huntsmen started to pursue the fox with any great interest. The 5th Duke of Beaufort is credited with 'discovering' foxhunting when after a poor day out stag hunting, he threw his hounds into a covert where they at once put up a fox. The ensuing chase so enthralled the Duke that he is said to have rid himself at once of his staghounds and turned his attentions solely to the art of foxhunting.

True though this story may be, the Duke was probably only discovering coincidentally what many other contemporary hunting folk were also finding out, namely that a fox on the run in the open presented a quarry finer than anything they had previously been pursuing. The only trouble was they had not the horses capable of hunting such a fast and nimble creature. Up until then any horses used for hunting had by necessity been sturdy plodders, up to good weights, who could trek all day through woodland and marsh. But what was needed now was a different steed, something which could keep up with hounds in full cry across country which required not only sustained galloping, but brave and accurate jumping. Thus more and more thoroughbred blood was introduced into the breeding of the hunter, and animals were consequently produced which gave rise to great pride of ownership. Which in turn led to boasts as to the prowess of particular animals, which in turn led to challenges being made between rival owners.

The competition was particularly hot in the country of Leicestershire, which because of the lie of its well drained land, immediately became the headquarters of foxhunting. And it was in this county that the initial 'matches' were regularly made between English huntsmen, the first one going on record in Leicestershire being the wager of 1,000 guineas struck between Mr Loraine Hardy and the Hon. Mr Willoughby in March 1790.

That matches such as these should become such a regular feature of English sporting life was only to be expected in a country so obsessed with *Equuo Caballus*. Ever since the invading Normans brought with them a conception of the horse as something other than just a beast of burden, both the monarchy and the populace had become enthralled by horse racing. As early as the middle of the 12th century races were being held at Smithfield, and by the 14th century the Plantagenets, particularly Edwards II and III were showing a keen interest in the sport, Edward III being personally responsible for the importation of entirely new blood lines. The Tudors all kept racehorses at Hampton Court, and Charles II, besides being responsible for the revival of the sport, not only owned many good horses and like Elizabeth I kept jockeys-in-ordinary, but on many occasions rode in races himself, and twice won the Newmarket Plate.

Soon 'matches' between huntsmen became a very regular fixture, the bloods often indulging in them on the way home after a dull day in the field. What is referred to as 'skylarking' now, namely the unauthorised jumping of fences on the way home, was to them a time to make challenges, prove their point, and win a few guineas. And as these matches became more popular, it was inevitable that sooner or later they would be run

In order to view these early steeplechases, many spectators followed the race on horseback, jumping similar or sometimes the same obstacles. (Arthur Ackermann & Son Ltd)

with more than just two contestants, and even more consequently that they would soon take the rough form of an organised sport.

Sure enough, as has been already noted, in the 1790s races began to be run with three or four participants, and by 1804 the first race over fences in which the riders wore distinguishing colours was recorded, when the Messrs Frisby, Bullivant and Day chased a straight eight miles from Wornack's Lodge to Woodwell. Six or seven years later (again, depending on the point of reference) saw the running of the first organised steeplechase over man-made fences, over three miles at Bedford. This race was the brainchild of a Mr George Tower, who designed his fences to be a 'fair test of genuine jumpers', and built them to the height at which they still stand today, namely four feet six inches, the only difference between Tower's fences and contemporary ones being that his had a strong bar running along their tops.

The other point worth noting here is that to qualify for the Bedford Steeplechase, the runners had to present 'certificates gained by being in at the death of three foxes in Leicestershire, the certificates being lodged with the Clerk of the Course.' This forges the link with present day point-to-pointing, since horses qualifying to race point-to-point or to run in hunter chases must have certificates signed by the Master of their hunt which declares them to have been hunted 'regularly and fairly' for the required amount of days. Ironically enough, although eleven horses were declared for the Bedford steeplechase, only two ran, thus making it less of a new-fangled chase and more of a traditional match. Even so, history relates it attracted a crowd of over 40,000 spectators.

Not surprisingly, given the excitement that watching horses jump seems to generate, in no time at all 'steeplechasing' had captured the public's imagination, despite the fact that in its infancy few concessions were made to the spectator. Races were generally run on the 'point-to-point' principle, namely in a straight line from start to finish, which afforded the spectator little chance of seeing anything of the race. Even so there was sufficient interest in the new sport by 1845 to encourage Henry Wright, a bookseller in the Haymarket, London, to publish his first *Steeplechase Calendar*, in which he accounted the number of courses over which steeplechases had been run since 1826, the year of one of the most famous of all 'matches', in which Captain Ross on a horse called Clinker by design all but killed his rival Captain Douglas riding a horse called Radical.

Wright's *Steeplechase Calendar* chronicled the sport since that famous chase, and listed the courses in use, which were few and far between. For until the year of Clinker and Radical's match, run over the same course from Barkby Holt to Billesdon Coplow as Charles Meynell had triumphed over in 1792, save for Bedford there were no other courses in regular use. Which meant that unless the contestant was thoroughly intimate with the countryside over which he was to chase, he could stand little or no chance of victory.

It was not until 1830 that the number of regular steeplechase courses increased from the singular to the plural, growing to a list of three which included a course of two miles out and two miles back from Hartlington Church to the obelisk in Wrest Park, Silsoe, in Hertfordshire, over which was run the inaugural St Albans Steeplechase, a race which was to achieve immediate popularity, so much so that for the subsequent nine years it was far and away the most notable date in the chasing calendar.

The race was the inspiration of Thomas Coleman, generally considered to be the father of steeplechasing, for it was unquestionably he who first really set about organising the sport.

Opposite, above: 1848 and the crowds were already swelling. The drop on this particular fence would appear to be at least ten foot. (Arthur Ackermann & Son Ltd)

Opposite, below: When Capt. Becher fell into the brook he was to immortalise, he remarked he never realised water tasted so foul without brandy. The jockey in the foreground here, however, seems to be saving his thirst for the beer tent. (Arthur Ackermann & Son Ltd)

Coleman had started his professional life working in the stables of Lord Arthur Wellesley, later to become the most famous Duke of Wellington, and then at Ascot for a Yorkshireman named Wetherall, qualifying hunters with George III's hounds so that they could compete in flat race plates for prizes awarded by His Majesty. He then set himself up as a trainer first at Brocket Hall, the home of Lord Melbourne, from where he trained successfully for five years, winning prizes all over the country, before moving to a farmhouse and stables in Lord Verulam's grounds at Gorhambury near St Albans. A man famed for living on his wits, he was also a skilful entrepreneur, as was proved by his purchase of the ramshackle Chequers Tavern in St Albans, which he razed to the ground, rebuilt and renamed the Turf Hotel, a hostelry that was to achieve an instant and enormous success.

Whether the attraction was the innovatory hot and cold water baths, the quite excellent food and wines served up by Coleman, or the gaming facilities it is hard to say. Possibly it was the combination of all three things that made the Turf Hotel one of the most famous sporting taverns in the land, regularly patronised by the likes of the inimitable Squire Osbaldeston — famed for many things, including the loss in one week at billiards of the then not inconsiderable sum of £3,000 — Prince Esterhazy, the prize fighter John Gully, General Grosvenor, Mr Tattersall, Colonel Charretie and Lord George Bentinck, who used to send Coleman horses in return for inside information.

The hotel also ran at over thirty stables, and Coleman began by successfully organising flat races in the St Albans area. But it was the growing dare-devil sport of steeplechasing which was on the tongues of the young bloods who did their drinking and gambling at the Turf Hotel, and although a theory runs that the famous St Albans Chase was the brainchild of some officers of the 1st Life Guards dining at the hotel, Michael Seth-Smith in his contribution to *The History of Steeplechasing* hypothesises somewhat oddly that Coleman 'would have been cunningly responsible for putting the thoughts into the young soldiers' heads.' Certainly there is little doubt Coleman not only organised the whole affair, but like many of the local tradesfolk, exploited the event to the full. At the inaugural meeting the town was overrun, and the public houses had to serve their beer by the bucket. The 'two miles out and two miles back' race was a huge success with the spectators, and was brilliantly stage-managed.

Determined that the competitors should not know which course to follow until 'the very last moment', Coleman had men with flags hidden in all the ditches, who were not allowed to reveal themselves until just before the 'off', when they were instructed to stand up with their flags raised in order to mark out the course. The promoter had also organised the race to be run in a horse-shoe fashion so that he could both start it and judge its finish by cutting back across country on horseback. Add to this the saddling-up of the sixteen runners in the paddock of the Turf Hotel and then a cavalry-like parade through the packed streets of the town, and it is little wonder why the St Albans Steeplechase was such a runaway success.

In fact it dominated the sport until December 1839, and did much to establish steeplechasing's permanence, as is shown by the fact that in the ten years since 1838 the number of organised meetings increased from a mere three to a healthy thirty-nine. It seemed to matter little that apart from running certain races 'there and back', no other concessions had been made at all to the poor spectator who, if he wanted to see anything whatsoever of the race, would have had to have dashed hell for leather on foot across rough country, or, as many did, follow the chase itself on horseback, sometimes even jumping the actual obstacles themselves. But for rural populations this seemed to matter little, because the steeplechase was a grand excuse for a day out eating and drinking and rubbernecking at the collected aristocracy, military and squirearchy.

There was also of course danger, that most necessary concomitant of all successful spectator sports. The obstacles facing horse and rider were formidable, solid stone walls, huge hedges, stiles with footboards, 'bullfinches', and plenty of water. The Vale of Aylesbury steeplechase, first run in 1835, was run over country intersected with very wide and deep brooks, which in the considered opinion of the race's instigators made it ideal racing country. So the bystander or follower of these early chases could expect to witness a lot of grief to both horse and man, and there are several documented instances of the deaths of participating riders. In fact in only the second running of the St Albans Steeplechase the death of a Mr Stretfield was noted, following a bad fall suffered by his horse Teddy the Tike while jumping a gate.

Because of this, and the accompanying cruelty to the competing horses, the new sport also had plenty of vociferous critics, who

considered steeplechasing to be barbaric and heartless. 'Nimrod', in real life one Charles Appleby (1778–1843), was perhaps the most ardent of the critics who put pen to paper. A man described as 'lifting the reporting of foxhunting to undreamt of heights', he was also an arrant snob, whose prose more often than not veered towards the purple. He adored the art of hunting the fox, but could make no connection whatsoever between it and the sport of steeplechasing, which in his more polite moments he dismissed as a mere cocktail. In his more venomous moments he described the sport as barbarous and repulsive, causing extreme danger to the horse or at the very least 'great temporary suffering'. He supposed that the heart of the famous chaser Grimaldi, who dropped dead after winning the 1836 St Albans Chase, although an organ of 'uncommon dimensions' ruptured at the moment of victory 'because it could not stand steeple-chasing.' 'Is it possible?' he went on to argue, 'that this barbarous pursuit can long continue to be a reproach to the character of Great Britain and Ireland?'

Robert Smith Surtees (1803–64), the creator of the inimitable

The 'Midnight Steeple Chase', meant to have taken place at Nacton near Ipswich in 1803 and thus to have been the first authenticated race. (Hulton-Deutsch)

John Jorrocks, also opposed the new sport. In *Mr Sponge's Sporting Tour*, published in the 1850s, Surtees wrote of steeplechases as 'crude ill-arranged things', as well as already seriously questioning the validity of hunters' certificates, and the competence of the 'misshapen gentlemen playing at jockeys', while around the same time an elderly foxhunter complained that unlike hunting, steeplechasing allowed the animal no chance of recovering his wind 'unless the poor beast falls', and finally denounced the sport as a 'bastard amusement, which no true sportsman who values his horse would countenance, and the sooner it is out of fashion the better.'

But the public disagreed, and although by 1839 the St Albans Steeplechase had oddly enough foundered, due to a sudden and inexplicable apathy, and in fact enjoyed its final running in that year (with apparently the winning owner being the only celebrant at the victory dinner), 1839 happily was also the year the first Grand National was run at Liverpool. Such was its immediate success that in the eyes of its supporters the future of the emergent sport must have seemed to have been secured by the events that took place in front of a vast crowd on the clear, bright and sunny afternoon of 26 February. Other courses had tried to establish the sport on a regular footing, but had met with only limited success. For example the very first enclosed course created specially at Bayswater, then a country area well outside London, a track which was described as 'perfect', being two and a half miles round, with a hill in the middle which provided spectators with a natural grandstand probably for the first time ever, suffered an acrimonious history, and had to be closed down in 1841, only four years after its opening.

Ironically enough, in light of its recent difficulties, in the year it staged the first Grand National the course at Aintree was also in trouble, although the track had only been laid out by its leaseholder Mr Lynn some ten years earlier. But Lynn's health and finances had simultaneously begun to fail, and the proprietor was beginning, like some of his later successors, to see Aintree as too big a drain on his resources, and regretted his financial involvement. 'I should have been worth at least £30,000,' he bemoaned in a letter to a colleague, 'if I had never had anything to do with it.'

Consequently a syndicate was set up and a race committee founded for the management and organisation of what was initially to be known as the Grand Liverpool Steeplechase, later changed in 1843 to the Liverpool and National Steeplechase, and entitled finally in 1847 simply as the Grand National.

It was an immediate sensation. Crowds of at least 50,000 people arrived at a course which was ill prepared for such an enormous invasion. Touts and their like had a field day, selling half-a-crown omnibus seats for half a guinea, and asking what they liked for a seven shilling grandstand ticket. The grandstand not unsurprisingly was consequently hopelessly overbooked, and all the smaller stands were 'crowded to suffocation'. Every vantage point, including even the chimney tops, was taken, and vast crowds gathered out on the course at all the most awesome of the obstacles, to watch the four mile race which was finally won by Lottery, and during which Capt. Becher immortalised a brook by taking refuge in it after a fall, and remarking with some displeasure that he never realised water tasted quite so foul without brandy.

Not everyone was happy with the spectacle of seventeen horses charging across such a formidable course, particularly since not all of them survived the experience. The *Liverpool*

Mercury made a sanctimonious plea for the banning of such races, comparing their appeal to that of cock fights, and bull baitings, and recommended that those who allowed their horses to run in such barbaric events should themselves be compelled 'to go through the purgatory of a steeplechase, with a sturdy driver at their heels to urge them over hedge and ditch . . . and when they arrived at the end of the steeplechase they should do penance in white sheets or horse clothes in the church until they confessed their iniquities and promised to be more merciful to their animals.' One week later however, a report appeared in the same paper noting that for the following year's National there were already fifty subscribers, and that the race was expected to be 'the most splendid ever witnessed'.

Even so, the growing popularity of steeplechasing was nearly its own undoing, because since the sport had no proper controlling body of its own, it wasn't very long before the rogues took over. There was too much quick money to be made for them not to move in. And move in they did. Well aware that steeplechasing had no administration remotely comparable with flat racing, already superbly governed by the Jockey Club under the aegis of one of racing's most impartial of umpires, Admiral Rous, the less scrupulous owners of steeplechasers totally ignored the vain attempts made by local stewards to administer some sort of justice. The stewards' hands were well and truly tied anyway, since their authority was only effective at meetings which came under their direct control. There was no liaison between stewards of different courses, nor between the clerks of those courses. If a jockey was suspended for foul riding, then that suspension was only effective at the course where the violation had occurred. 'Ringing' was rife (the substitution of one horse similar to another for the purposes of a betting coup), as was not trying, suspicious riding, foul riding, fraudulent entry, and the forging of hunters' certificates. And there is a famous case on record of one unscrupulous owner parading a broken down 'dog' in the paddock in order to obtain long odds on his real runner which meanwhile was waiting down at the start. Racecourse stewards were openly defiant and disobedient, and were known when challenged to defend themselves 'with disgusting and insulting language'.

And since the Jockey Club stoically refused to recognise steeplechasing, there was no method, as there was in flat racing, of 'warning off' trainers, jockeys or owners who had committed serious offences. Therefore the more unscrupulous members of the steeplechasing fraternity quite cynically and openly started to exploit every loophole open to them, to the severe detriment of the sport.

And the sport could well have died the premature death so many were predicting for it had not the National Hunt Committee been formed just in time in 1866. In the late 1850s there was every chance that steeplechasing, which had been in such good health in the '30s and '40s might disappear altogether, not so much because of the continued opposition it was still meeting from so many quarters, including (which is surprising to this day and age) many foxhunters, but more because of the apathy and blatant dishonesty of the sport's organisers. Also, the unpleasant and unfortunate disagreements witnessed by the public at many meetings did the image of steeplechasing little good, likewise the regular and successful betting coups organised in handicaps on lowly bottom weights with no previous 'form'. Incidents such as the Clerk of the Course at St Albans excusing his failure to offer the winner of the seller according to the conditions of the race because 'darkness had fallen and most people had gone home' did little further to enhance the sport's already doubtful credibility.

The National Hunt Committee, comprising of sixteen men, most of whom were members of the Jockey Club, and one of them, Mr W. G. Craven, a Senior Steward, at once set about trying to clean up steeplechasing's act, turning its attentions first to the vexatious task of properly defining the eligibility of 'gentlemen riders', the incorporation of hurdle races in the *Steeplechase Calendar*, the adjudication (by Tattersalls) of disputed bets on steeplechasing, the introduction of a weight for age scale for chasers and hurdlers, and a reciprocal arrangement between France and England regarding the prevention of disqualified owners and horses from running in either country.

But despite their sterling efforts at reforming the image of the sport, by the end of the 1860s the critics were still giving tongue. One or two had reformed their opinions, most notably the correspondent in *Bell's Life* who noted with pleasure the size and scope of reforms already carried out on a sport which only recently had 'surely sunk to the lowest depths of degradation' and had been 'synonymous with robbers and with no recognised laws to protect it'. But thanks to the good works being carried out by a few 'good men and true', steeplechasing was no longer the ' "illegitimate" despised thing it was', but now ranked 'proudly side by side with other and ennobling pastimes'. The majority of critics, however, remained steadfastly unimpressed, particularly the purists who could see no way of including it in the list of 'legitimate' sports. To them it was unnatural because it was not the test of a true hunter, but rather a contrivance for the carrying on of betting transactions on races which were seldom if ever won by the favourite, due to the roughness of the riding, the scrimmaging of the horses, and the more than questionable tactics of their pilots.

It can be argued that it was the adoption of this attitude which led to the birth of the 'renegade' sport of point-to-pointing. Vian Smith in his book *Point-to-Point* believes that around the late 1860s many amateurs, or 'gentlemen riders', disgusted by the cruelty of the sport and the tactics of the participants, or believing that too much emphasis was being put on speed rather than on the jumping abilities of the so-called hunter, withdrew their support, preferring to retrench and re-consolidate their links with the hunting field.

Lord William Lennox expressed the prevailing attitude most eloquently when he wrote:

> 'If, during, or at the end of a hunting season, gentlemen like to try the merits of their respective horses over four or five miles of a fair country, there can be no possible objection to such a proceeding – on the contrary it is an amusing and harmless recreation. But when horses that have never followed a hound, ridden by professional jockeys, are brought out to gallop three or four miles over a racecourse with stiff stone walls, strong post and rails, awfully large artificial brooks, hurdles, thick fences and broad ditches, the whole feature is destroyed. Instead of its being a test of a good hunter, it degenerates to a mere gambling racing transaction.'

This was the Corinthian ideal epitomised. For the belief was that steeplechasing was a natural adjunct of hunting, and even more importantly, that the sport should be an entirely amateur activity. Organised 'professional' steeplechasing was the antithesis of this doctrine, for out hunting the horseman could take his own line and wherever and whenever possible avoid exposing himself and his horse to unnecessary dangers. In steeplechasing there were no such alternatives. Horses, rarely properly qualified in the hunting field, were asked to jump a line of fearsome obstacles, and if they tried to refuse they were hard beaten or spurred into them, with the result that many animals were killed or badly maimed. The belief therefore ran among the purists that if gentlemen wished to race their hunters, then they should do so only under the auspices of their hunt.

Out of this schism was thus born the sport of 'point-to-pointing'.

OFF AND RUNNING

'Out of discord comes the fairest harmony'

Controversy surrounds the exact year the sport got under way. According to Colonel Lyon, one of the sport's earliest chroniclers, 1885 is claimed as being 'the year of the first recorded point-to-point'. Michael Williams, the doyen of contemporary annalists, and the greatest expert on the subject, disagrees, finding evidence in the records of the Worcestershire Hunt that on 2 March 1836 the first Worcestershire Hunt meeting took place 'over a course on the west bank of the Severn from a point at Frieze Wood by the Old Hills on the Madresfield Estate of the Earl Beauchamp, to the centre of the Lower Powick Ham, where Capt. Lamb's Vivian ridden by Capt. Becher won.'

If such a thing were possible, it would seem that both parties are right. Because whereas there most definitely was a 'point-to-point' meeting on the Earl of Beauchamp's estate in 1836, it would appear that there was only one race run at it and in the following year only two. In fact it wasn't until 1851 that at any of these very occasional hunt-organised assemblies were more than two races run, and from 1864 to 1883 there were no recorded meetings at all. Which is probably why the 1880s must be given credence as the proper beginning of point-to-pointing, since this was the time the first fully fledged meetings were noted. The validity of this date is underwritten by the fact that in 1882 the National Hunt Committee issued its first set of provisos concerning racing 'between the flags', the first of many such strictures intended to prevent its country cousin growing too big for its boots.

Nonetheless, the sport gained real momentum in the 1880s, although ironically enough in form point-to-point racing returned to that of the early and now much despised steeplechases, namely races run in straight lines across natural country for the amusement of a handful of gentlemen. But the renegades were content nevertheless, for Mammon had not been given best, and the Corinthian ideal was still intact.

The main difference between 'professional' steeplechasing and racing 'between the flags', lies in their dissimilar locations. Steeplechase courses are by and large town and city orientated, since the sport relies on the attendance of the public, and the public may be more easily persuaded to go racing if their hippodrome is only a short walk or ride away. Point-to-point courses, however, rely on landowners' and farmers' goodwill, since the races are invariably run over a third party's land. In the early days of the sport, when 'bee-line' or 'horse-shoe' races were the vogue, the course might run over fields and through woodland owned by several different parties, so the promotion of goodwill in the chosen locality was paramount from the word go. The public was not a consideration initially, since one of the first rules passed by the National Hunt Committee when it started to take note of point-to-pointing forbade the taking of

A racecard for the meeting of the Worcs. Hunt in 1903. (John Hopwood)

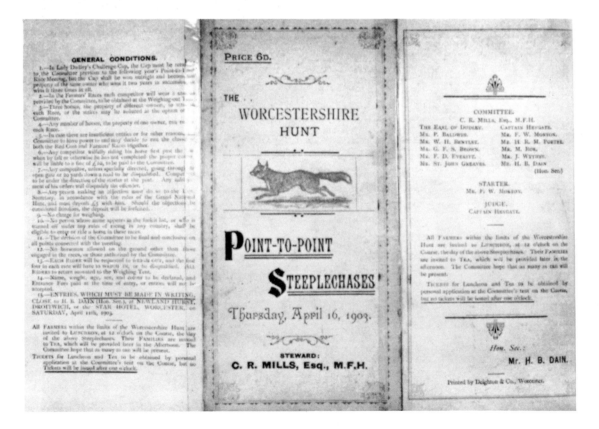

Oxford Undergrads at a college point-to-point at Stratton Audley in 1901. The habit would seem to be the same then as now – namely to gain as many admissions as possible on one carpark pass. (Simon Blow)

gate money. So if the spectators were not going to help swell the hunt coffers, then basically they and their needs could be ignored. Little wonder so many of the early meetings were such chaos, leading Thomas Quarrel in his *History of the Worcestershire Hunt* to write of the Hunt's first meeting in 1883 that it was attended 'by an enormous crowd of people mounted, who rode alongside and behind the competitors, with the result that much confusion occurred, and the Judge had great difficulty in deciding the winner of the Red Coat race.' Judges today still frequently experience great difficulty deciding certain winners, but at least they cannot proffer as their excuse that they failed to read the finish because of their view being obscured by crowds of mounted enthusiasts.

The sport grew with quite astonishing speed, and its rapidly increasing popularity did not go unnoticed by the National Hunt Committee, who had not yet managed to set their own house in entirely good order. In fact the decline that had set in during the year 1876 had not been fully arrested, mainly because the committee itself was experiencing trouble in framing both its own definition and the rules of the game, while certain clerks of certain courses were blithely refusing to pay prize money over to the winning owners, and stewards everywhere were continuing to act like tin pot dictators. At one notorious meeting at Wye in 1895 it was noted that from a long and formidable list of stewards, not one of them finally bothered to attend the races. There were also complaints, as reported by a sub-committee in 1882, that the sport was going 'soft', due to the decrease in the size and type of jump, with the result that the 'accomplished chaser has no chance of proving his superiority over the half-educated racehorse, hence the almost entire withdrawal of the former from a sport which fifty years ago was all jumping, (but) is now all galloping.' So it was hardly surprising that the N.H. Committee should be more than a little concerned by the rapidly increasing number of point-to-point meetings and their fast growing popularity.

Although for some years both forms of steeplechasing managed to co-exist fairly harmoniously, the authorities nonetheless still felt it necessary to begin to regulate racing between the flags. In 1882 they decreed that 'point to points need not be advertised, and horses having run in such races should not be disqualified from running at meetings under National Hunt Rules, with the proviso that no point to point course must be defined'. Not long after, in 1889, it was further decreed that each hunt could have only one meeting a year, but no course could hold more than one meeting without express permission. There must be no admission charges, no race of less than three miles, and most importantly of all and most controversially, there must be no prize awarded greater than £20. This last proviso alone led to considerable and prolonged disagreement between the administrators of the two sports, an argument which has been carried forward to the present day.

Of course it was absolutely vital that proper order should be brought to point-to-pointing, since without a rule book all sorts of abuses would very soon have been rife. It is probable that despite the great and undoubted enthusiasm which there already was for the amateur game, without supervision the lunatics would have taken over the asylum, and the sport would have gone to the wall. Times were already changing, and before long hunts would be forced to take proper note of their dwindling resources, and look for alternative ways of raising revenue. Point-to-pointing was to provide a sizeable chunk of their income, and so the days for ignoring the needs of the attendant public were fast dwindling.

Not so much a steeplechase, more of a novice hurdle. The second at Pytchley in 1911. Formal hunting dress was then de rigeur *for all races.* (Simon Blow)

For whatever fun it might have been for the competitors not to know the course they were to ride until they were escorted to a starting point sometimes up to six miles away from the assembly point and directed towards the finishing flag which often was not even visible until the race was half run, the wretched public can have derived little lasting pleasure from such meetings. Some commentators, not entirely unpatronisingly, have remarked that few complained because the majority of onlookers were rural labourers, and a day out with the family and a picnic provided sufficient satisfaction. If that had really been the case, it is doubtful that the hunts would have ever felt the need to bother about improving conditions at all for the public, and spectators would still be watching races run in a bee line for the sole diversion of the horses' and the riders' connections.

Changes came, slowly but surely, as the organising bodies became aware both of the need to cater for the public and the need to improve and control the quality of the sport. However, it is well known that things have a habit of getting worse before they get better, and the case of point-to-pointing proved no exception. For a while in the 1890s things got more than a little out of hand, and the sport became so dangerous that several hunts abandoned their meetings altogether for several seasons. People were becoming horrified by the sight of so many injured horses, many of them fatally so, and the prospect of riders returning after fiercely contested races covered in blood and with their habits in rags. This was hardly a very satisfactory refutation of the criticism the Gentlemen had but only recently levelled at the Players.

So the racing became more formalised. Courses were no longer kept as a secret until the 'off', nor were men hidden in ditches with flags to indicate the directions of the contest only once the horses were off and running. The obstacles and the route were now marked out with fixed flags, initially only as a recommendation as to which line to follow, leaving those with more derring-do still to jump where they liked, but finally, due to continuing abuses and accidents, it became compulsory for all riders to jump the same obstacles and follow the same course 'between the flags'. Of course those participants with more than their fair share of hair on their chests announced that this was 'cissifying' the game, arguing that the bravest should still be allowed to choose their own route. After all, this was a gentleman's pursuit, an amateur sport requiring no unnecessary qualifications and regulations. But conformity won the day, and shortly afterwards not only did all the riders have to follow the same course, but they also had to turn for home at the halfway point which was also marked by a flag. At long last the neglected spectator could witness not only the start of the race, but possibly, if he was quick, also the most important part, the actual result.

Needless to say, not all the courses fell into line. As late even as the 1930s there were still dissidents, among them, according to Michael Williams, the Equitation School at Weedon, who in 1935 were still refusing to disclose any advance information about how and where the course was to run up until the day of the race itself. And not only that, they still ran their races in a 'very stiff line' straight across country for 3¾ miles, while the Puckeridge at Brent Pelham throughout the Thirties included in their course post and rails, ditches, and combination jumps, and the High Peak at Flagg Moor in 1936 were still running their mixed light and heavyweight Members' Race over a four mile course which included thirty-six stone walls.

Not everyone wanted to get into line and in fact there was strenuous opposition to any changes being made to point-to-point courses. A very strong lobby maintained that if races were no longer run over natural country but over regulation birch fences instead, the sport would simply become nothing but steeplechasing in miniature. They were right. That is exactly what the sport did become. But contrary to these Jeremiahs' gloomy prognostications, this imposed uniformity did not kill the sport off, but only helped to strengthen it.

There were heated disagreements too about the type of horse which should contest point-to-points. Up to the First World War, the thoroughbred racehorse took little part in races held in deep country. There the well subscribed races were contested by traditional hunters, farmers' cobs, 'small' horses (i.e. the offspring of small mares and thoroughbred stallions) and even ponies of 14.3 hands or less, who apparently raced over the same distance and jumped the same obstacles as horses two to three hands bigger. And quite understandably, since such races must have been the most enormous fun for and of the most intense interest to the local country community, the participants resisted any proposed changes, most of all the increasing infiltration of the dreaded ex-racehorse into their ranks. Feelings on this subject ran very high, and over twenty years later the people who had enjoyed their sport at grass roots were found still to be protesting against the way things had changed.

The toll of equine casualties in the Great War was grievous: millions of horses meeting terrible deaths in action, hundreds of thousands often by simply drowning in the mud.
(Imperial War Museum)

According to a letter published in *Horse and Hound* in 1939 they maintained that point-to-point races were 'designed for hunters carrying hunting weight and ridden by hunting men. Unfortunately they have changed considerably. A large number of ex-racehorses are now competing, and point-to-points have progressed a long way towards becoming merely bad race meetings.'

But the sport was bound to change, not just because the organising bodies required a certain uniformity in order to make the administration of this type of racing more practical, but because events overtook it, most particularly the mass carnage that followed the assassination of the Archduke Franz-Ferdinand at Sarajevo in 1914.

For in the calamitous fighting which followed, not only were millions of men and boys most grievously lost, so too were millions of horses, shot, blown up or simply and horribly drowned in the mud. While National Hunt racing continued, point-to-pointing closed up shop, unable to survive the loss of its horses and its gallant young riders. When peace was declared, the sport took a long time to recover, even though meetings were being organised and held by 1920. But the entries were few, and the crowds unremarkable. Oddly enough though, the newly formed governing body, the Master of Hounds Point-to-Point Association, assembled in 1913 to frame the sport's own charter, gave 'pointing' more by accident than design a shot in the arm just when it needed it most. It decided to allow ladies to compete.

Or perhaps to put it in a more correct perspective, there was nothing in the new rules framed so assiduously by the Association which denied the ladies the right to do so. And so the ladies quite rightly took full advantage of exploiting a loophole which the more conservative gentlemen trusted would very soon and not before time be blocked. But this was the age of the enfranchisement of women, and having helped so admirably during the war on the land and in the factories, the distaff mood was distinctly bullish. So among other things, they began to ride point-to-point, and not only that, they did not choose to compete merely against each other, they confronted the opposite sex head on.

It is not clear how many of these dashing ladies rode side-saddle and how many rode astride. What is certain is that they met with immediate and considerable success: Miss V. Selby-Lowndes winning the lightweight race at the West Street

A Ladies' Open in 1932, two astride and two across. Many ladies maintained it was easier to jump side-saddle. (London News Agency Photos Ltd)

Left: Miss Marion Carrington Smith, aged 16, about to saddle up at Northaw Herts in 1932. From 1930 until 1967 ladies were declared ineligible to ride except in races confined to their own sex (this happily was not the case in Ireland). (S & G Press Agency Ltd)

Harriers' meeting in March 1929 (riding side-saddle incidentally), Miss J. M. Magee won against the men in East Anglia, as did Miss Jean Sanday in Cheshire, and the Misses Melvill and Spooner in the West Country. Other ladies to ride with great success in East Anglia included the Misses Reeve and Parry, and Mrs Cooper Bland.

There is little doubt that this took the 1920s man by surprise, since the idea of ladies not only riding against men but actually being capable of beating them had appeared ludicrous, to say the least. Predictably enough, moves were soon afoot to alter the rule book, and in April 1929, one week after Sylvia Spooner won at East Cornwall on her famous pony Mohun, the Master of Hounds Association called it a day, forbidding ladies henceforth to ride point-to-point against men. The Jockey Club and the National Hunt Committee must have heaved a joint sigh of relief, because it was directly against their canon to allow ladies to play any part in racing at all, other than as owners, or of course as grooms.

Under the new ruling, however, ladies were still allowed to take each other on in point-to-points, an idea somewhat impishly attributed to men who didn't fancy the notion of

Spectators at the Fernie. The fair sex appeared then to enjoy dressing up to go pointing, rather than the modern habit of dressing down. The key worn by the lady second left would appear to be for her cine-camera. (Simon Blow)

coming second to a woman. The ladies took no time in retrenching, and very soon ladies-only races were a regular feature of every good point-to-point racecard.

There had actually already been ladies-only races well before this stricture was passed in 1929. The date of the very first one is another of these areas of controversy, some settling on the meeting of the Bucks and Berks Staghounds at Sonning in 1925, where Mrs Weatherby won on a horse called Reggie, while Michael Williams once again begs to differ and states quite categorically that the first authenticated ladies' race was in fact run at the South and West Wilts Hunt meeting held at their old course at Motcombe, as early as 1921. To back up his claim, he even quotes a living and trustworthy memory:

> I recall that the favourite was Slauntha, who was saddled up by Geoffrey Phipps-Hornby. In this race Lord Stalbridge, the Master of the South and West Wilts, rode behind the competitors in case any of them should need assistance. To the best of my recollection, he was left far behind!

Williams reports that the race was won by the aunt of Anneli Drummond-Hay, Lady Jean Douglas-Hamilton, 'who rode her horse Cavalier II side saddle and went like the wind.'

The other boost point-to-pointing got during the 1920s was the involvement of the then Prince of Wales. The man who was briefly to become King Edward VIII and sadden his more ordinary subjects by his enforced abdication was, when Prince of Wales, an enormously popular figure with practically everybody, and most particularly with the working classes, who saw him both as a glamorous and charismatic hero, albeit a bit of a rebellious one. But that only added to his appeal, and the amalgamation of his good looks, his debonair quality, and his dash were a very heady mixture, so much so that when he decided to ride in a humble point-to-point in the West Country, thousands of people from that part of the world with no interest in the sport whatsoever invaded the little course at Wrangaton in the hope of seeing a royal victory.

They were disappointed. For as a jockey the Prince was blessed with more courage than skill, so much so that one particular fence at Tweseldown in Hampshire used to be pointed out as 'the

HRH The Prince of Wales, waving to a royal auntie from the back of Pet Dog, at Chipping Warden in 1921. Never the most skilled of riders, the Prince nonetheless was instrumental in bringing the sport to the general public's notice (note the 'natural' fence). (The Press Association Ltd)

fence where H.R.H. usually comes to grief'. Even so that day in the West Country H.R.H. managed to stay on board and finish second on his little mare Miss Muffet, beaten only from the last fence.

His luck was definitely not in again when he rode at the Harkaway Club meeting at Chaddesley Corbett in 1928. Once again the course was packed with the non-cognoscenti, wrongly dressed and ill-equipped for a winter's day in deepest Worcestershire, and once again they failed to witness the hoped-for royal victory. H.R.H.'s mount refused in the first race when in the lead, sticking her toes in at the fifth fence and shooting the Prince off over her head, and in the open nomination race when the royal jockey was once again leading, his mount slipped going into the Open Ditch and came down on her side in the mud. Nonetheless the Prince remounted and managed to finish a creditable fourth, although it is not apparently recorded how many runners there were in all, and how many finishers.

Although the Prince never enjoyed the racing success the present-day Princess Royal has, his association with the then modest and to many unheard of sport of point-to-pointing suddenly made what had been regarded as an eccentric activity

The first fence of the Prince of Wales Cup at the Army Point-to-Point, Aborfield Cross. Again, note the 'natural' fence. Regularisation had yet to come. (S & G Press Agency Ltd)

enjoyed only by the military, the country gentleman and the farmer into front page news. All at once the sport was by appointment to the Prince of Wales, and it was immediately elevated into the ranks of 'respectable' pastimes. And all this a good quarter of a century before the Queen Mother was to dignify National Hunt racing by her enthusiastic patronage.

The last development of any great note before the outbreak of the Second World War, and one which was finally to mould point-to-point racing into the shape in which it more or less is today, was a political one. The Master of Hounds Point-to-Point Committee and the National Hunt Committee had by 1934 increasingly been begging to differ concerning the administration of the sport. So much so that at the AGM of the Master of Foxhounds Association in May of that year Lord Lonsdale proposed the setting up of 'a Select Committee . . . to consider the whole question of the Point-to-Point committee of the Master of Foxhounds Association.' In other words, the National Hunt committee wanted centralisation, all the better to control the waywardness of its renegade but ever-growing country cousin.

In particular the administration needed to be tidied up, and the sport given the uniformity the National Hunt Committee had hoped the Master of Hounds Point-to-Point Committee would impose on it. So a Joint Advisory Committee of three members of the National Hunt Committee and three selected representatives of the Masters of Foxhounds Association was formed. Its purpose — to make more rules, naturally. And so with the creation of a special appendix, Appendix C, in the National Hunt Rule Book, as from July 1934 point-to-point racing came directly under the government of the National Hunt Committee, where it remained until 1969, the year the Jockey Club decided to place it under its direct jurisdiction.

Major new regulations included the creation of a body of twenty-three course inspectors, whose job it was to approve the courses and inspect the fences. Fences had been getting smaller and weaker by the years, and odd though it might seem to the layman, the easier the fence the more dangerous it may be, because 'clever' horses know they can all but ignore them, and inexperienced but 'hyped-up' riders are tempted to take quite unnecessary risks at them. Much better that the fences be well and firmly built so that both the horse and rider will have to think twice about taking risks at them. There was a snag to

bringing the fences up to standard, however, and that was the stiffer the fence, so it was thought, the smaller would be the entries. Many courses had been attracting large and therefore lucrative entries by insuring their fences were small and feeble, while it was noticeable that at the courses where the fences were larger and more properly packed entries were considerably smaller.

Even so, sense prevailed, because most organising committees realised that if the sport was to survive and flourish, then it must improve. Huge fields consisting mainly of nondescript runners finally do not attract good crowds. The really good crowds, ones that will keep returning to the sport, are those who appreciate good racing and jumping, so it was in all the courses' general interest to make sure that their fences came up to the required standard.

The new ruling body also took a long hard look at the system of stewardship, and very soon made it perfectly clear that it would not tolerate the appointment as officials of men chosen for their social status rather than their knowledge of racing. There was far too much of the old boys' network act going on for

A fine action shot of the Maiden at the Garth in 1938. The fences at Aborfield by now resemble today's obstacles. The Old Guard resented the changes, and continued to lobby for 'more natural fences'. (The 'Topical' Press Agency Ltd)

the committee's liking, and although there is still criticism levelled at stewards for this self-same failing even nowadays, it has to be admitted that by and large the supervision of point-to-point meetings is infinitely better than it was before the last war. Then the style was often to favour the local horse in a tight finish and to over-rule any blaggardly objection from the runner-up. Michael Williams, in one of his delightful 'overheards', quotes one such example.

1st Steward: I say. Shall we have that blighter so-and-so up?
2nd Steward: I should bloody well think not. He's one of ours!

Most importantly, the Advisory Committee introduced a ruling that 'No horse which, since January 1st of the current hunting season has been trained by a licenced trainer, unless the horse be his own property, or by an unlicensed person (other than his owner, groom, or the proprietor of the stable from whence the horse has been hunted), shall be eligible to be entered in a point-to-point steeplechase.' It also defined the people it considered ineligible to ride. This list, with the exemption of lady riders, and since 1990 grooms, still holds good today, much to the chagrin of a certain lobby who feel a complete review of this list is long overdue.

No other major reforms were recommended before another world war once more savagely curtailed the entertainment, although the old order believed most earnestly that their sport was being ruined by the interference of 'busy-bodies', and that the 'naturalism' of point-to-pointing should have been allowed to continue untrammelled by the strictures emanating from an ever-enlarging rule book. Some tried to contain the threat which was being posed by the introduction of so many thoroughbred horses into the sport by suggesting the minimum weight in men's races be raised from 12½ stone to 13 stone, which would balance the scales in favour of the sturdy hunter type. Others wanted the weight reduced to 11½ stone, while some even suggested the introduction of handicapping. All these recommendations were listened to and then studiously ignored.

As indeed were any opinions proffered by the old Masters of Hounds Point-to-Point Committee. By 1937, only three years after the invention of the Joint Advisory Committee, it was being recommended that the Masters Committee be dissolved, since the Joint Advisory Committee was seen to be coping so well. But more realistically perhaps it was because the National Hunt

Committee had made it abundantly clear it would be happier to deal with only the one authority. The motion was carried unanimously, and with a 'hearty vote of thanks for their extremely valuable services in the past', the Masters of Hounds Point-to-Point Committee was then consigned to oblivion.

Undoubtedly this was considered by the old guard to be the end of their sport as they knew it. They considered the conformity which had been imposed on their sport to be unwarranted, and not at all in the spirit of things. It was their unshakeable belief that to be true to themselves horses racing point-to-point should run over the sort of fences encountered in the hunting field, that 'good hunters should win races, and clever horses deficient in pace should be able to score victories over the pure and simple speed merchants.' Their dismay at what had befallen the sport was epitomised in the criticism levelled at point-to-pointing by the *Daily Telegraph*'s hunting correspondent, Capt. Lionel Dawson, published in *The Horseman's Year* in 1946:

> 'Point-to-pointing has become a species of bastard race-meeting, run for profit and with prizes competed for by horses principally kept for the purpose, and barely qualified as hunters, frequently, whenever conditions permit, ridden by jockeys who seem to get about quite a lot.'

Happily, the public found no such fault, and the number of meetings increased with each season, so that by the end of the 1930s there were nearly two hundred fixtures, attended by crowds which consistently ran into the thousands. In fact at one meeting of the Barlow near Chesterfield, a crowd of 20,000 was estimated. It is impossible to ascertain whether or not this is a true figure, since because no charges for admission were allowed, a head count could only be roughly reckoned from car parking fees, and the sale of racecards, allowing three to four people a car, and two people per racecard. What is indisputable, however, is that attendances were rocketing, and contrary to the old guard's belief, what was attracting people to the sport was the dramatic improvement in the quality of the racing, which in turn was due to the improved quality of the participating horses and the notable achievements of the leading riders.

So much so that many National Hunt supporters began to entertain serious worries about the success of something it had seen only as a much, much poorer cousin. As crowds were rapidly increasing at point-to-points, so they were diminishing at

Opposite: Probably the greatest Corinthian of them all. The late galloping Major Guy Cunard, who totalled 268 winning rides since World War II, seen here winning on Ferncliffe at the Middleton Hunt Point-to-Point in 1964. Few ever dared to 'come up' on his inside. (Jim Meads)

All In The Family

There are several families who have participated continuously in the sport with each generation, none more notably so than the famous and popular S.W. family of the Dufosees. (Photos courtesy of the Dufosee Family)

Left: The first of a dynasty. Harry Dufosee on Royal Wilts at the S&W Wilts meeting in 1926.

Above left: His son Peter Dufosee being presented by HM The Queen with the trophy for winning one of the divisions of the inaugural running of the Coronation Cup at Larkhill. The other division was won by none other than Ted Edgar.

Above centre: Peter Dufosee battling it out with a member of another illustrious point-to-pointing family, Michael Tory.

Above: Peter Dufosee's son John, winner of 79 point-to-points and now one of the leading livery yard owners. (Frank H. Meads)

Right: Jason, John Dufosee's son and the latest family recruit, winning on Monkton Rill, a mare owned and bred by his grandfather Peter.

Part of point-to-pointing's tradition has always been the picnic. This was the start of a day out at the Pytchley in 1911. (Simon Blow)

certain regulation steeplechase courses, with the result that more than just the occasional steeplechase meeting was being quietly dropped·from the Racing Calendar. Commentators gave the reason for National Hunt's decline in fortunes as the cheapness of admission to point-to-point races, rather than bothering to examine what was wrong with the order of their own house, namely that they themselves were sanctioning too many race meetings. There just simply were not enough good horses to contest them, nor enough paying spectators to attend them.

With the meteoric rise in point-to-pointing's popularity, so the benevolence all but disappeared from the National Hunt Committee's despotism. It had always adopted a somewhat baleful attitude towards its poor country cousin, as can be seen in its consistent refusals to raise the ludicrously low level of prize money, and its small minded but mercifully unsuccessful attempts to place restrictions on consistently successful horses. They were determined to try and keep the upstart well and truly in its place, but despite all their efforts at limitations the sprout mushroomed.

It was not surprising. The 1920s had seen some good horses, and some fine riding, but come the 1930s there appeared probably one of the best point-to-pointers of all time, O'Dell, the famous grey horse owned by Major Harold Rushton, the Master of the Worcestershire, who won for his owner over forty races including two Liverpool Foxhunters, a race which was then still run over the full Grand National distance of four miles. The Thirties saw some other quite outstanding pointers too, including Hopeful Hero and Duty Paid, both Irish bred. It was exceptional horses such as these that started attracting the bigger crowds, as did the exploits of their pilots: cavaliers such as Major Guy Cunard, who was just beginning his famous hot streak, the characterful Ryan Price, destined after the war to become a noted if somewhat controversial trainer, and who once rode five winners in one afternoon, the Holland-Martin brothers Thurston and 'Ruby', the latter of whom used to race-ride in a monocle, Peter Scudamore's grandfather Geoffrey Scudamore, Lord Grimthorpe, who gave his name to the race known as the point-to-point Grand National, and Major Ian Straker, whose two sons both became riders of note.

There were also several future N.H. trainers including Major Calverley Bewicke, Arthur Stephenson, Neville Crump, Fulke Walwyn and Ken Oliver, E. W. W. Bailey, Capt. Harry Freeman-Jackson, and the famous West Country family of Dufosee, three of whose members, Harry, Tony and Peter were all riding winners, not to mention many brilliantly talented ladies, the most popular and famous of whom were Miss Sylvia Spooner, the leading woman rider of the time, and the Irish mother and daughter team of Mrs Evadne and Miss Diana Bell. Evadne Bell rode all of the twenty wins scored on her best horse Rattles side-saddle.

Little wonder then the crowds that made their way to their local point-to-points were enthralled. And little wonder the numbers were steadily increasing. Now that the public was being catered for, however primitive the amenities, going point-to-pointing offered unbeatable value. For the price of a car park ticket and a racecard, in the Thirties probably no more than five or six old shillings (25 or 30 pence), a family of four could have a splendid day out, particularly once the latter part of the season was reached, namely late April and May. The tradition of the point-to-point picnic was long established, having started probably as early as the late 19th century when the sport had begun to take a hold in the countryside, and when the rural workers' only holiday would perhaps be a day out with the family watching the gentry racing their best horses over walls and ditches, so by the Thirties point-to-point fans were well used to making a day of it. Point-to-pointing allowed for far more informality than its parent sport, and this was one of its main attractions. If the weather permitted, long unhurried picnics could take place on the grass, dogs and children could roam around quite freely – sometimes a little too freely perhaps – old friends could be caught up with and new friendships forged. Friendly rivalries could be renewed and niggling old scores settled – usually quite amicably. Farmers were entertained by the hunt, the hunt was entertained by the thought of the money it was making, and on a fair day everyone went home happy.

Much of which still holds true nowadays. Certainly as we write, at the beginning of the 1990s, the first time visitor to Larkhill, Flagg Moor, Chaddesley Corbett, Chipping Norton, or Lemalla need have no worries for his safety. The deeply rural racetracks where the point-to-pointers run have no interest for the coaches full of the drunken hooligans who terrify so many formal racetracks. There are no untoward or violent incidents reported at the meetings held in the folds of the Devon hills, or the cultivated splendour of the Duke of Beaufort's course on his estate at Didmarton. Sometimes on Bank Holidays, the more fashionable courses are host to a few too many drunk, noisome and foolish Hooray Henrys, but generally speaking the worst that can befall the spectator at a point-to-point is that he or she might get frozen, drenched or stuck in the mud of the car park.

It's an institution peculiar to these islands, and one which has evolved from both our sporting and our social history. And despite the constant attempts to make it conform and fall into line, point-to-pointing has still somehow managed to retain its uniqueness. Vian Smith attributes its success, its survival and its importance most elegiacally to its grass roots connection:

Point-to-point racing grew into the memories of countrymen; for boys became men and remembered what boys had seen and what they had seen as boys became more daring and startling and worth remembering as soon as they were too old to remember clearly.

Any meeting fulfilled an important function, giving entertainment and excitement to those whose winters were long and dark. For young and old in remote corners of England, Wales and Scotland, 'the races' were not Derby or Grand National, but the point-to-point. These rural workers belonged to generations which lived on crumbs and crumbs can seem a feast to the starving.

This is what point-to-point racing is all about. It is not only a minor meeting, too small for some Sunday newspapers to find space for. It is the past as well as the present. It is an old man's memory of holidays when holidays were rare; a young man's memory of what his father and grandfather have told him. Affection has grown out of half-memories so that a country district regards its point-to-point meeting as quite different from any other race-meeting of the year.

This affection is one of the qualities which make point-to-point racing different. The other quality is absolute amateurism in a society increasingly professional.

That was written over twenty-two years ago. It seems to hold as well now as it did when first it was penned, with the exception, perhaps, of the final paragraph. Because although it is true that our society has become even more increasingly 'professional', particularly in the way it enjoys its recreation, it is regrettably arguable as to whether or not point-to-pointing's amateurism is quite as absolute now as it was then.

GENTLEMEN AND PLAYERS, AND GENTLEMEN AT PLAY

'It seems that win-win-win by almost any means is the order today. When I was young, things were much more amateurish than they are now. I remember before my first point-to-point my father told me to keep to the right, as horses always run out to the left. I do not think the hunting point-to-point fraternity knew that it was possible to put the whip in the left hand. Anyhow, on that occasion we had to jump in and out of a lane. I was duly on the right and the horse next to me on my left turned sharp left down the lane, taking the entire field with him, so I won.'

Thus wrote Ulrica Murray-Smith, former Joint-Master of the Quorn for twenty-six years, in the columns of *Horse and Hound* in 1989. Mrs Murray-Smith, besides being one of the most notable huntswomen of recent times, was also a bit of a pathfinder between the flags in the Thirties, since she is still remembered now even in those far off days as stepping out of a light aircraft at the old Chiddingfold course in Surrey just in time to be legged up on to a horse which then duly proceeded to win the Ladies' race under her.

But however revolutionary her means of arrival may have been at the racecourse on that notable day in 1934, judging from the tenor of her written reminiscences, there is nothing else particularly radical in the Hon. Mrs Murray-Smith's credenda. A remarkable horsewoman and notable huntress, she subscribes to the school of thought that believes 'if a horse, be he racehorse, jumper or eventer, goes very well, this in itself is very satisfying.' She also believes, and is certainly not alone, that much of the traditional 'good sportsmanship' so especial to the world of

Gentlemen working at their play. The Judge's wagon at the Belvoir in 1923 included from right to left The Earl of Londesborough, Bobbie Clayton Swann and Captain Bertie Sheriffe. (Simon Blow)

competitive riding, has long gone, and that in competition today acts of chivalry are practically non-existent.

Many of her contemporaries were people of a similar disposition, pronouncing as far back as the Thirties and the Forties that the sport was no longer nearly such fun, and was becoming far too competitive for its own good. On the other hand as many voices were being raised in contradiction, voices which belonged to those who believed just as sincerely that to satisfy the appetite of a rapidly growing public, point-to-pointing must be run on more uniform lines.

Judging from the history of the sport, there seem always to have been these two opposing factions, the one determined to improve the overall standard of both the racing and the participating horses, and the other equally determined to preserve its 'amateur' status, and to prevent it from simply becoming 'steeplechasing in miniature'. Ever since George Tower's first 'organised' steeplechase in Bedford, a race which he framed with the deliberate intention that it should be for hunters and not for thoroughbreds, there has been consistent

and often confrontational argument as far as racing between the flags goes, as 'to what is and what is not proper'.

For instance, in the Thirties, Lord Lonsdale, appalled by the apparent mollification of point-to-pointing, was heard to complain that the situation was fast becoming 'perfectly ridiculous' – on attending a certain point-to-point he once overheard someone complain that 'the fences were too big, and that there was a ditch on the take-off side' – while at the very same time others were complaining that because of the increasing 'professionalism', point-to-pointing was losing its individuality, becoming too streamlined, and as a result races were becoming ever more hard to win!

Whether it was considered more difficult to win races because of the ever-growing number of thoroughbred horses taking part, because of the improved standard of the competitors' riding, or because of the steps which were being taken to standardise the courses themselves, is not made clear, although it was known the old guard did publicly consider that the interference by the National Hunt Committee with point-to-pointing was crass and motivated by jealousy. Yet ironically enough, as has been already indicated, it was the National Hunt Committee's famed 'interferences' which assured that the sport retained its amateur

The softer the fence the greater the risk. The hatless but certainly not gutless Miss A. Covell brushing aside the opposition to win at the Chiddingfold and Leconfield in 1948. (Miles Bros)

profile, since it was they who defined the constitution of a 'professional' rider, and it was they who had introduced the all-important rule forbidding any horse which had been trained in a professional yard since a certain date in the season from competing in point-to-points. In those days the date was 1 January of that year. Nowadays it is the first day of the previous November.

In order to try and understand the two widely differing attitudes entertained by those participating in one and the same sport, it is perhaps necessary to consider the ambivalent attitude which the British have always adopted towards 'professionalism'. It is not a readily admired trait, considered by many traditionalists to be an unwelcome American by-product. For a long time the people who ran things in these islands would generally have been of the type inclined to applaud the efforts of a one-legged ballerina having a go at *Swan Lake* more than an overly professional two-legged one dancing it perfectly correctly.

That world, a twilight one now, was divided strictly into Gentlemen and Players. What was important was not that 'you won or lost, but how you played the game'. And in racing between the flags that meant that although you might ride into the enclosure as the winner on another fellow's horse, you let the chap who came in second on his own home-bred take the Cup, as happened in a Bar point-to-point once, at Coombe near Malden, when the Hon. Alfred Lyttelton, later the Colonial Secretary, declined the cup after winning the Heavyweight race, recommending instead that it should go to the runner-up, Mr J. G. Butcher, QC, MP, whom Lyttelton deemed to be 'worthier of it as he had entered and ridden his own horse'. In those days, gestures such as that were often made (some would argue because they could then be afforded), and Bad Sports were Bad Pennies. Bad Sports did ungentlemanly things, such as lodging objections. And if and when they did, it was a one hundred per cent certainty those objections would be overruled, simply as a matter of principle.

For sport was then considered to be a pastime, a leisure pursuit, an amusement. It was not considered as a means to an end. Triumph and Disaster were both to be treated as impostors, and what mattered was neither winning nor losing but taking part. This was considered to be the correct attitude, whereas the 'professional' one was incorrect, since a 'professional' was out not merely to take part, but to win.

If you were a member of these privileged ranks before the Second World War, then doubtless it must have been fun to have been a participant, and fun it had to be, since fun was certainly then considered to be the all important concomitant of good sport. And the best and most unadulterated sport was still unquestionably to be found in the field, which was where the gentlemen came out to play, particularly on horse. In fact it was such an addiction that the British abroad could not do without it, forever organising amateur race-meetings and even full scale point-to-point meetings in far flung outposts of the Empire, as long ago as pre-First World War, when and where doubtless the races between the flags were not organised and run under any official set of rules, but under the famous British agreement of gentlemen.*

It is therefore not ridiculous to suppose that many of those who objected to the regularisation of their sport throughout the Thirties, Forties, and Fifties were either those returned from

---

* The brother of Lady Waechter (huntsman and Master of the North Ledbury for forty-nine years) and a friend actually managed to start and run a pack of hounds when they were both POWs in the First World War.

Above: Proving that you can take it with you. Prize-giving at the Cavalry School Point-to-Point at Lahore, India, 1912.

The winner of the Heavy-weight ponies (12 st) race at the Cavalry School meeting taking the last well clear.

abroad, or their relatives, or perhaps even their offspring, who would have been brought up to respect what they considered to be the traditional British sporting values. Understandably they would be opposed to any changes which they might consider were being made just for the sake of change, for they required their world to be a place made tolerable still by its traditional amusements.

Arraigned against them were those who were dedicated to the overall improvement of the sport, the highly suspect 'professional' element, motivated it seemed not by an altruistic desire to put more into the sport but actually to take out from it. These were those who cared more for racing than for the art of venery, those much despised 'players' who only hunted to qualify their horses, and who, on the few days they were out, were to be witnessed pussyfooting their thoroughbred racers round the lanes and roads when hounds were in full cry and the 'gentlemen' were flying the raspers.

By and large, these 'professionals' were professional in attitude only. They were not 'shamateurs', just people who believed that if a thing was worth doing, then it was worth doing properly. Some were simply less traditionally minded members of the gentry who were determined their sport should survive and grow, and saw the only way that could happen was for it to be properly organised, while others came from the ranks of the newcomers to the game, the artisans and tradesmen whose children had enjoyed good hunting with the Pony Club, and who now wished to graduate to point-to-point racing. But these good people were not as advantaged as the more traditional owner, having neither large farms nor estates upon which to keep and train their charges. When the time came to prepare their horses for the coming season, the rich farmers and retired military simply handed their horses over to their farm hands and their grooms. The butcher, the baker and the garage proprietor had no such good fortune. They had to do it themselves.

Or, as their fortunes improved, have others do it for them. And here lies the sport's major anomaly. For as it has been indicated, under the Rules of Point-to-Point Racing, it is strictly forbidden to have horses in training in a professional yard after a certain date (nowadays 1 November) if they are to be eligible for the forthcoming season. But before going any further, the question must now be asked as to what exactly constitutes 'professional' training, or more precisely, the word 'professional' itself.

> **professional** adj. Of, belonging to, connected with, a
> profession; following occupation (esp. one usu. engaged in as
> pastime or by amateurs) as means of a livelihood; making a
> trade of something usu. or properly pursued from higher
> motives; maintaining a proper standard, businesslike, not
> amateurish. Disparagingly applied to one who 'makes a trade'
> of politics, etc.

From that *OED* definition, it is a question of money and choices.
Either it is the maintenance of proper standards, or the making
of a living (or even worse, a trade) from something more
properly pursued from higher motives. But what is abundantly
clear (besides the fact that this has to be one of the most *snobbiste*
determinations in the whole lexicon) is that if someone is paid
for a service, then they are professional. And that, at least as far
as point-to-pointing was concerned, was where the famous
cookie crumbled.

For as the sport grew, and ownership became more cosmo-
politan, so the methods of training horses for point-to-point
racing changed. Most of these new owners had neither grooms
nor farmhands to whom they could simply hand their horses,
and while many of the less affluent learned very well how to
keep and train their new charges at home, others with better
lined wallets and less patience looked for someone else to do the
donkey work for them.

Except whoever they chose must not be a 'professional'
trainer, otherwise their freshly bought horses would be ineligible
to race between the flags. An answer was soon found, which was
that there was nothing in the rule book to say that owners whose
intention it was to run their horses in point-to-points could not
stable their charges in hunter or livery yards. After all, not
everyone had an old cow byre or derelict barn they could
convert into stabling. Since many of the new owners came from
towns, they had to keep their horses somewhere, and livery
yards existed for that purpose. And since point-to-pointers had
to qualify in the hunting field, there was nothing that was not
meet and proper in them standing at livery in a hunters' yard.
Particularly if the said horses earned their hunters' certificates
from the address at which they were stabled.

And so it came to pass that for those who could not or would
not Do It Themselves, and yet who wanted the thing done
properly, it became the practice to stand their horses in
professional livery yards, which was permissible since they were

not deemed to be professional training yards. Not unnaturally within the sport this provoked, and still does, a great deal of heated debate. The subject of livery yards and the role they play is dealt with in Chapter 6, but in the meanwhile suffice it that the argument against livery yards is pretty much a glasshouse one, because the enraged traditionalists who were the first to declare such a thing just 'not to be on', were usually following the same code of practice on their own home ground, namely the employment of professionals to look after their horses.

Most houses who could afford to keep a number of horses to go point-to-pointing employed grooms. And those grooms were paid to feed, look after, exercise, school and gallop their employers' racehorses. Likewise the farmhands given charge of their rich masters' strings may not have been employed specifically for that purpose, but they were still being paid to do precisely the

The picture of a 'professional' amateur, and one who went on to become one of the most successful women in NH racing: Monica Birtwistle at the Holcombe in 1948, during which season she was later to become Mrs Tony Dickinson.
(Associated Press)

same job as the lads and lasses in a 'professional' livery yard. And between these big private yards, with their numerous horses, their paid help, and probably any number of amateur jockeys willing to ride out for them, provided their owners knew their business, there would really be very little difference between them and the 'professional' livery yard. The only people genuinely entitled to adopt a holier-than-thou attitude were the genuine DIY owners, who kept just one or perhaps two horses and had no paid staff to help them whatsoever.

In their infancy, however, the stabling of potential point-to-pointers at livery yards met with strenuous opposition. Even today north of the Humber, where by tradition change is a lot longer time a-coming, the 'professional' livery yard is practically unknown. However, further south, there is room nowadays happily for both forms of 'training', even though 'professional' livery yards are still not officially recognised as being other than as generally described.

But it can be argued that the sport owes its present rude health because of rather than in spite of this infamously increased 'professionalism'; for it is in nobody's interests, least of all that of the participating animals, for an activity such as racing horses over fences to be run in blissful semi-ignorance. There is no benefit to be had from horses being produced to run half-fit, incorrectly trained, and quite possibly unsound. The consequences are inevitably disastrous and often tragic. A greater awareness of what it entails to train horses to win races can only be beneficial to the sport. If this attitude earns the sobriquet of 'professionalism' then so be it, particularly if that is taken to mean the 'maintenance of a proper standard' rather than the 'making of a trade of something properly pursued from higher motives'.

Whatever, had the purists won the day, and point-to-pointing remained in the hands of the elite, then there is little doubt that the sport would not have survived. For the end of the Second World War saw many changes, the most notable being the immediate election of a Labour Government. And Britain's new governors were not at all well disposed to those who indulged themselves pleasurably in blood sports. There had been plenty of antipathy expressed in between the world wars towards hunting, but Ramsay MacDonald's first two Socialist administrations in the Twenties were too short lived to effect any legislation, and the mind of the so-called 'National' government of 1931–5 was on matters of far greater national importance.

So it fell to the Attlee administration of the Forties to re-invigorate the hunting controversy, which it did with a vengeance, encouraging the introduction of private Members' Bills which sought specifically to outlaw the hunting of deer, badgers and otters. There had been organised opposition to hunting since 1924, when The League for the Prohibition of Cruel Sports, nowadays known as the League Against Cruel Sports, had been formed, but up until World War II its membership had never risen above 3,000. It was, however, and always has been, more than generously endowed, particularly by the bequests and legacies of rich animal lovers, far more than the British Field Sports Society, which was formed in 1930 as an immediate reaction to the RSPCA's pronounced support for a Bill designed specifically to outlaw deer hunting. By 1939 the BFSS had approximately 10,000 members. By 1949, the year a Private Member's Bill was introduced whose aim was the proscription of all forms of hunting with hounds, except foxhunting, and thus the year when the BFSS faced its greatest challenge, its membership soared to well over 100,000, a figure which has yet to be beaten.

It is not the purpose of this book to enter into a dialogue concerning the pros and cons of field sports. But since point-to-point racing has always been inextricably linked with hunting, it is necessary to take note of these events in order to see how the sport was effected by the outcome of this debate. For it was a widely held belief amongst hunting people that were this particular Private Member's Bill to be passed, legislation also banning foxhunting would inevitably follow. And if so, it was considered that one of the knock-on effects most certainly would have been an end to point-to-pointing.

In all probability, had the anti-blood sport faction won the day, and foxhunting ultimately been banned, it is doubtful whether it would indeed have sounded the death knell for point-to-pointing. It would have just popped up through another hole. The same pertains today, with the contemporary concern for the future of hunting. The attention of today's racegoing point-to-pointers is constantly being drawn to the need for them to support the BFSS if they wish to guarantee the survival of their sport, but truth to tell, were there indeed to be a total prohibition on hunting, all point-to-pointing would need for its survival, were the Jockey Club to continue to act as its controlling body, would be a change in the rules concerning the eligibility of horses. If there was no hunting, there would be no need to qualify hunters.

As it happened, despite a highly contentious debate, the 1949 Private Member's Bill was defeated by 214 votes to 101, the most influential speech coming from, surprisingly enough, the Socialist Minister of Agriculture, Mr Tom Williams. He concluded:

> 'In my view, the prohibitions in this Bill have no economic foundation, and the humanitarian aspects are greatly exaggerated if not wholly misconceived.
>
> Since this party has been given the power to govern the nation, I believe we have a record of achievement of which we ought to be proud, and I hope that at this moment we are not going to forfeit the goodwill we have so rightly earned to go down in history as a party anxious to abolish the pleasures of others.'

Even more unpredictably, a Government-sponsored committee, under the chairmanship of Mr J. Scott Henderson KC, set up to enquire as to whether hunting was a cruel or an effective means of controlling animals designated as pests, in 1951 found in favour of foxhunting, and spelt an instant reprieve for over 400 hunts.

Nevertheless, despite these resounding victories, the more sensible huntsmen were left substantially wiser by the events. For a considerable length of time they had been lobbying their more arrogant members to cease making their absurdly exaggerated boasts as to their courage, and to stop publishing their constant and ridiculous claims of having run thirty or even forty mile 'points' (i.e. the distance in a straight line between the start of a chase and its end), since such lunatic and dangerous pretensions made for extremely bad public relations.

In fact many hunts became much more introspective, a likely result of having taken fright at the ferocity of the opinions held by those who opposed them. The need now was for support, and the right support could only be gained by tact and tolerance. And it became more and more evident to those who bothered to look that the loyal support they so desperately needed was to be found right on their doorstep, among the ever increasing crowds which were now attending the hunts' point-to-points.

For by the crucial year of 1949, racing between the flags was enjoying easily its best post-war year. In 1948 there had been 136 meetings. One year later the number had risen to 179. It was also the year Major Guy Cunard began his astonishing run of championship successes with a total of twenty winners, a record then for the most in one season, and the crowds that came to watch him and his confederates were as big and sometimes bigger than in the last golden years before the war, and certainly often made a mockery of the poor crowds then being attracted to many minor National Hunt meetings. But the composition of the crowds going racing point-to-point was now quite different, with far more people being attracted out to the rural meetings from the towns, their attendance at what had seemed previously quite inaccessible venues made possible by the advent of the cheap family saloon car. After the deprivations of a war, sport had become a form of national celebration, and despite the handicap of petrol still being rationed, the population took to the roads, and as a consequence chanced upon forms of entertainment of which previously they had been ignorant.

Point-to-pointing certainly benefited, although what the town dwellers made of their first excursions into these rural enclaves is hard to imagine. The uninitiated must have felt as though they had strayed into some sort of secret society. But they cannot have been that dismayed, or deterred, because they kept on coming back for more, so much so that before very long a substantial percentage of loyal point-to-point supporters had no connection at all with the countryside, least of all with hunting.

Paradoxically enough, this tacit support worked in the hunts' favour. With costs rising all the time, and unable any more to depend on enough large private donations, many hunts were becoming more and more fund conscious. They could hardly go cap in hand into the towns and cities looking for support without risk to life and limb, and yet here were people from those very towns and cities, some of them possibly even hostile to hunting, lending their financial support to their local hunts by attending their annual point-to-points. This is one of the peculiar qualities of a point-to-point meeting: the fact that in the self-same crowd there can be enthusiasts who share a mutual love of racing between the flags and yet whose views on blood-sports will be diametrically opposed. It is possible to surmise that amongst the many spectators who gather at the modern point-to-point courses there may be those who not only are totally disinterested in the future of hunting, but many probably who have no idea at all of the inter-connection that exists between the sport they follow and the following of hounds.

The advent of the modern and more militant style of 'Anti' demonstrator had an interesting rebound effect. The adoption of more brutal tactics, such as physical harrassment, the placing of bombs in horseboxes, acts of vandalism and desecration, including the infamous profanation of the 10th Duke of Beaufort's grave at Badminton, an incendiary attack on an MFH's house, and the firing of a horsebox belonging to the late Dorian Williams while he lay dying of cancer, all helped to alienate public opinion against the perpetrators of the violence, and certainly contributed to making up the minds of those who until then had been sitting somewhat uncertainly upon the fence. The end result was not just a battening down of the hatches. Rather it was the birth of a greater awareness by the hunts of their responsibilities and of the vulnerability of their former position, one which had so very often been sustained previously through arrogance and presumption.

To survive, it was vital for the hunts to show a more 'human' profile, and the efforts of the newly created public relations department of the BFSS in the Seventies made considerable gains in this direction, through their successful attempts to improve the media coverage of the associated field sports. But most of all it can be argued that since man has to live by both sorts of bread, many hunts owed their survival not so much to the untarnishing of the sport's image, but more to the support and the funding of its subordinate, the annual point-to-point.

REGULARLY AND FAIRLY

In the early days of steeplechasing a popular fiction existed that the horses were hunters; and grooms and fellows used to come nicking and grinning up to masters of hounds at checks and critical times, requesting them to note that they were out, in order to ask for certificates of the horses having been 'regularly hunted' – a species of regularity than which nothing could be more irregular.

So wrote Robert Smith Surtees in 1850 in what many consider to be his best book, *Mr Sponge's Sporting Tour*. And from this illustration it can be seen that the debate about qualifying has been going on as long as the sport itself. To the initiate, it is one of point-to-pointing's great mysteries, particularly since it is a protocol with no hard and fast rules. Consequently, unless beginners have their wits about them and find out exactly what is expected of them, they may well, as they say in the shires, come most frightfully unstuck.

The experienced point-to-pointers know the drill full well, because they do it annually, and if they always qualify their horses with the same hunt, they will know not only the protocol, they will also know the dodges. They will know for instance whether their racehorses are properly welcome in the field, and may be hunted as other horses, or whether they are expected to keep a lower profile and simply be seen at the meet and not heard of much thereafter. These are the aspects of qualifying which can only be learned by experience. What novices can learn in advance is how many times they are expected to hunt their animals before the 1st of January, which is the earliest date upon which the necessary Hunters' Certificates for the forthcoming season may be signed and issued.

On enquiring they may be told that their particular hunt likes to see qualifiers out anything up to at least eight times, depending on how the Master of the Hunt wishes to interpret the rule which stipulates that 'point-to-point steeplechases are confined to horses certified by a Master of a recognised pack of foxhounds which have been regularly and fairly hunted in Great Britain during the current hunting season'. Nowadays in order to qualify, horses must have their certificates signed by the Master of the Hunt with which they have been out hunting, since some rather loose wording of this particular rule previously allowed the more unscrupulous to obtain certificates from MFHs who had never clapped eyes on the animals in question let alone ever seen them 'out'.

As far as qualifying itself goes, it really is a case of *chacun à son gout*. Some hunts are infinitely more strict than others, insisting that qualifying horses must hunt actively up to at least six or eight times, and that they must stay out for a minimum of three hours. And just to make sure that no one cheats, certain of these zealots issue qualifying riders with tickets, which are then only signed by a hunt official after the qualifiers have stayed out for the required period of time. No Hunters' Certificates are issued until the correct amount of signed tickets are produced.

At the other end of the scale are the hunts that only require a nominal amount of appearances, perhaps as little as two or three. Some hunts, truth to tell, would be quite happy if those qualifying, having paid their subscriptions, were never seen again beyond a few token appearances at the meet. Others of their kind allow qualifiers to follow hounds for the first hour or so of the day, provided they do not, to put it euphemistically, get in the way. Thus the infamous 'wretched hang-dog crowd of qualifiers on the road' referred to so disparagingly by one D. W. E. Brock forty years ago in his book *Point-to-Point Racing* are not always 'riding about on the roads' voluntarily, but often because they have been thus instructed. Certain types of Masters have indeed been known to enquire of qualifiers whether it was not time for them to say goodnight, should any of them be found going first rather than a distant last. One thing which does seem indisputable is that the worse the hunting is the longer the qualifier will be expected to stay out.

All this is something which the debutant may only discover by trial with hopefully little attendant error. It is always well worth swallowing pride and asking exactly what is the form. But not of the Master nor any of the hunt officials. They are bound by the rules of the game to supply a coded answer. The persons of whom to make the necessary enquiries are those similarly engaged, that is to say other qualifiers. Although hunts tend to be cliquish, the ambition of most members and subscribers is for their hunt to keep running on its well laid lines, so enquiries made by any newcomers will usually be met with courtesy, and the debutant qualifier will soon be pointed in the right direction.

It is absolutely essential for all beginners to understand what is expected of them. If they are expected to hunt their point-to-pointer extremely regularly and very fairly, and by this it is understood they are not to loaf around all morning in the lanes, nor sneak off back to their horseboxes the first moment the Master's back is turned, then those qualifiers must make sure that both they and their horses are up to the required standard. The wise Master, and the sensible Hunt Secretary know full well the danger of hunting thoroughbred racehorses, particularly those who have joined the field after a lifetime racing under Rules. The sight and sound of hounds will excite them, as will the spectacle of any amount of horses suddenly taking off at the gallop. Their instinct and their training is to take those other horses on, and the hunting field is no place for a steeplechase.

Some old or retired racers take to hunting as if born to it, in fact many racers who have gone over the top are apparently greatly rejuvenated by a period in the hunting field. But if racehorses are to be hunted up front then it is better that they are in safe, capable and sensitive hands. If not, even the better mannered racehorse can be too much of a liability in the field once the huntsman blows away and hounds give tongue.

So newcomers must not feel they are being made unwelcome should they be politely but well advised not to 'get in the way'. If they feel they are not being given a good run for their money, because they really want to hunt their horses, then they must prove their worth initially by following hounds tactfully and unheeded. The experienced Masters, or watchful Members will invariably take note, and qualifiers may well consequently be made more welcome. However, there is a strong school of thought which considers that if it is indeed the ambition of certain parties riding point-to-point horses properly to follow hounds, then for this privilege they should pay a full hunting subscription. The real hard liners believe that all qualifiers notwithstanding their aspirations should pay a full subscription.

As it stands at present, those qualifying their point-to-pointers are generally asked to pay the hunt's minimum annual contribu-

Jill Dawson qualifying her wonderfully successful mare Sweet Diana with the Southwold, and obviously enjoying every minute. (Jim Meads)

tion. Again, there is no across-the-board figure for this, some of the smaller hunts charging £60 a horse per season, others upwards of £250, as opposed to expecting qualifiers to pay the full hunting sub which can be as much as £1,700 plus VAT to subscribers living outside the Quorn country (and which incidentally only entitles them to two days' hunting a week).

To find out exactly what they are expected to pay, newcomers need only ask their Hunt Secretary. The Hunt Secretary needs to be a man of exemplary temperament, for his post is usually an honorary one and his job the most discretionary. Given that the newcomer's Hunt Secretary is found to be such a fellow, hopefully also of an amiable disposition, upon being asked he will soon volunteer the amount of the newcomer's expected subscription, and the number of days the horse should be seen out. Should anyone wish to qualify more than one horse in that season, then an arrangement can be made with the Hunt Secretary. Newcomers should not be shy of asking, as this is a standard procedure. In fact most Hunt Secretaries adopt very realistic attitudes to the business of subscriptions, and provided initiates beard their Secretaries at opportune moments – not say when they are trying to collect the caps at a Monday Meet, or ten minutes after they have returned home following a hectic red-letter Saturday – they will find them veritable mines of invaluable information concerning the all important protocol of hunting, including not only demeanour in the field, but also such things as 'cap' money, and other ancilliary donations, and whether or not qualifiers are expected to give over and above the usual amount. For purely racing matters, however, the person to ask is not the Hunt Secretary but the Hunt's Point-to-Point Secretary, who will usually have to be contacted by telephone, as he or she may not always be a huntsperson. It is, in fact, very important to mark and learn who is exactly who and why out hunting.

Naturally the quality and 'wantability' of the hunting affects the size of the subscription. One source allows that 'hill packs will do anything for £50', and another that a typical subscription in his area for an average hunt is £270 per person regardless of whether the subscriber intends to qualify one horse or ten. To qualify a horse with the smartest pack in Leicestershire, or with the Duke of Beaufort's Hunt, will cost around £300 a horse, in contrast to a full subscription to the East Cornwall for two days a week at a mere £60 per horse. In some parts of the country, the problem of what to charge qualifiers has been partially solved by the neighbouring hunts forming a cartel and agreeing between themselves as to exactly what the minimum subscription should be.

There is in fact a case to be argued for a set national point-to-point subscription. After all, it is supposed, horses are qualified to run between the flags regardless of where they are hunted. An animal qualifying for £50 or less with, for example, the Banwen Miners, should its owner so desire is perfectly entitled to compete in Mens' or Ladies' Open races anywhere in the country, against horses owned by those who have had to pay probably six times that amount. A same-for-everyone subscription, it is said, would at once remove such an irritating anomaly.

Opponents of this cause refute such a proposal, since they seem to consider any interference with hunt finances to be tantamount to an invasion of privacy. Hunts are autonomous bodies, and as such are allowed to design their own constitutions. Any suggestions from the outside world, particularly from

ancilliary organisations such as the Point-to-Point Owners'
Association as to how their subscriptions might be regulated are
not exactly welcome. This sort of thing is generally taken to be
the thin end of a wedge. And one thing hunts are peculiarly
averse to are thin ends of wedges.

The hunts' attitude is more understandable when viewed in
context. Many of their more reactionary members consider
subscribers qualifying point-to-pointers to be interlopers, claiming
that the art of venery has been debased by the presence of
racehorses and their jockeys in the field. Furthermore they
consider that qualifiers are allowed out only by courtesy of the
hunt, that the annual point-to-point meeting is run by the hunt
for the benefit and enjoyment of the racers, and as previously
discussed, were there no hunting, there would be no point-to-
pointing. Therefore it is up to the hunt to decide what the
qualifier should be expected to pay. These in fact are the very
people who if they had their way would enforce the maximum
and not the minimum subscription on those wishing to qualify
their horses.

Happily, while many hunts may have several such members,
they are no longer running the show, and the more even minded
huntsmen value the contributions made to their hunts by the
sensible qualifiers. And the word 'sensible' is used here quite
purposefully, because it must be said that for every red-necked
huntsman there is an equally brass-necked qualifier, who sees
hunting only as a means to an end, namely to get a Hunter's
Certificate signed as quickly and as painlessly as possible. Not for
this type of qualifier the observation of protocol, or a show of
respect for the sport. These people consider hunting owes it to
them, just as wrongly as their opponents suppose point-to-
pointing owes it to hunting.

Once the niceties of qualifying have been marked and learned,
the question to which debutants must next address themselves
must be a proper reading of the instruction 'fairly'. If it is to be
assumed that time out qualifying is not to be spent loafing and
'coffee-housing' around the lanes, then an understanding should
be reached of how to hunt a point-to-pointer. There are, as is
only to be expected, two schools of thought concerning this
procedure. The more traditional one says that there is no harm
but only positive good to be had by letting the point-to-pointer
take a proper place in the hunting field, the theory being that the
hurly-burly of the chase is good experience for the young horse

and a harmless one for the more experienced campaigner. Moreover, there is absolutely no doubt at all that the regular and fair hunting of a point-to-pointer in the weeks before New Year's Eve contributes greatly to the animal's good health and subsequent fitness.

Others disagree most positively, arguing that how horses are expected to behave in the hunting field, constantly checking and queuing at jumps which are then often taken at a trot and canter, and the sort of obstacles they are required to face, namely tiger-traps, post and rail, stiles and the like, can only be detrimental in the training of the modern point-to-pointer. Besides that, there is the very real risk of exposing the potential steeplechaser to quite unnecessary hazards, particularly since the modern hunting field has been made so dangerous by the abundance of flints turned up by the plough, and by the widespread and sometimes quite indiscriminate use of wire, barbed and otherwise. There is little doubt that it is always highly regrettable for a horse whose real aim is to go racing to suffer an injury out hunting, particularly a wound which could perhaps with better guidance have been avoided.

The choice should perhaps finally be dictated by both the type of horse and the type of rider. A novice horse ridden by an owner who is not going to compete on him but is just simply qualifying his charge would best be advised to keep a low profile and not ask either himself or his horse to perform anything beyond his known capabilities, whereas an experienced horse ridden by the person who is going to race-ride it might well benefit by flying a line of hedges and enjoying the thrills of a red-letter day. What is essential to bear in mind is that however racehorses are to be hunted, whenever possible they should be qualified by the beginning of January. For it is usually after Christmas that the weather worsens, and if, with only a month or less to go before the 'off' it is discovered a horse still needs another four days out before he earns his certificate, these required days can suddenly be in short supply when the ground starts to freeze. So as with most things, it is a case of much better safe than sorry.

A few hunts make it easier for qualifiers by allowing days out 'cubbing' to count. Others view such a notion with alarm, and make their feelings on the subject well known to any newcomers. Even though regular subscribers do not have the inherent right to go cubbing, but must ring their Master first to gain the necessary permission, it is still somewhat hard to understand the

The superbly attired David Naylor-Leyland qualifying Reynard's Bow, on which Michael Felton won at Lockinge in 1987, with the Quorn. (Jim Meads)

reasoning behind not allowing these days, if granted, to count, since during the cub hunting season, the number of mounted followers is considerably smaller than it is when the season proper opens, so accordingly the presence of any qualifying parties would be far less felt. The hours out are similar to those of foxhunting days, although start times are much earlier in the day, and if the sport is good there is every chance for horses to be hunted fairly and regularly.*

Luckily nowadays qualifiers can take their choice before they pay their money, whereas before, when point-to-pointing was in its infancy, as was horse transportation, those wishing to hunt so that they might race as a rule were able to look no further afield than the ranks of their local hunt. Today thanks to the tremendous improvement in communications and the growth of

---

* It also helps ease the burden on the land if qualifiers are disposed of early rather than later on.

livery yards, the experienced owner of point-to-point horses might well qualify his horses where it is most suitable, the suitability being governed by the chosen hunt's attitude to qualifying, and even more importantly, by the number of its so-called adjacent hunts, a point which will be amplified later when the various categories of race are examined.

Having chosen which hunt, and having learned its particular protocol, debutants have only one other ritual to which they must conform, and that is the matter of dress. It has become far too common a sight to see the more insensitive qualifier, just as hounds are moving off, turning up late dressed in an old pair of riding-out breeches, an anorak, and an uncovered skull cap, with an ungroomed horse half covered in an exercise blanket. And it has to be said much to their own discredit, that many a Hunt Secretary, rather than lose precious cap money and perhaps even future subscriptions, at moments such as these develops a convenient attack of blind-eye. Even so, the Hunt Secretaries are less to blame than the ill-dressed qualifiers. Regardless of the fact that nowadays they have to pay their dues and are no longer out hunting by invitation only, qualifiers, like every other hunt subscriber, are expected to dress correctly, and if that means black jacket, white hunting tie or 'stock', butcher boots and a velvet cap, then so be it. In less formal hunts, 'ratcatcher' is perfectly permissible, but that means not any old riding-out clothes but a tweed, whipcord or Melton cloth jacket, breeches, and a bowler hat or velvet cap. The principles of hunting dress are harmony and conformity. These are house rules designed for convention, and must be accorded due regard by all concerned parties.

The qualifier's horse must be equally well presented, groomed to a sheen, and with mane either plaited or pulled and laid to one side. All other parts, visible and not so visible should be well scrubbed and clean, and tack should be immaculate. If the initiate's horse is to be qualified from a livery yard, tips on the expected standard of turn-out can be gleaned from the proprietor or staff, although as is to be expected the notion of what is acceptable and what is not varies enormously between yards. Some yards consider horses and riders should be as well turned out on the lawns at a meet as they are in the paddock on race days, while others see no point in burdening the owner with yet another cause for extra expense.

The final *caveat* is whenever possible not to hunt a qualifying horse at the more popular meets. Nowadays it will not be welcomed out on Saturdays more or less anywhere, unless the weather has been unusually inclement in November and December, thus limiting the number of suitable days, and the Hunt Secretary is an understanding man. So for the good of all, qualifiers should seek to take their horses to the smaller mid-week meets called at distant villages and windswept cross-roads. Because they are of a lesser size, and because they are held in the more remote corners of the hunt's country, these meets tend to be considerably less formal, and therefore considerably more fun, particularly for the less experienced qualifier.

The next required item at this stage of the proceedings is, of course, a suitable horse.

A Horse, a Horse

'There are only two sorts, the plain and the coloured'.

Oscar Wilde was talking about women, but the very same could be said of horses when it comes to racing, that there are the plain and the coloured, although how the potential purchaser distinguishes between those that can and those that cannot race is a question which has been vexing experts for well over two thousand years.

In fact the only certainty in racing is that money cannot buy winners. Money most certainly facilitates the purchase of the better kind of animal, but as every racegoer knows, horse racing has more than its fair share of expensive-failure stories. A rich man nowadays may pay upwards of £30,000 for an Irish point-to-pointer with 'form', only to find once it has been shipped to and stabled in England the animal is quite inexplicably incapable of winning even the most modest of Open point-to-points.* His neighbour on the other hand may have a small and unfashionable home-bred which is still running unbeaten after six races. Mercifully racehorses are great levellers, otherwise were it just a matter of money, there would be no sport.

There are various categories of horses likely to race between the flags. Starting with the youngest, these may be either horses

* Note C6 from JC Regulations
The Stewards of the Jockey Club wish to draw the attention of owners who have purchased Irish Point-to-Point horses which have won, as to their eligibility to participate in the Point-to-Point races in this country. Owners are advised that the majority of Irish Point-to-Point races are 'Open' races (i.e. horses qualified with any recognised pack of hounds). For example, those horses which have won a Novice or Maiden Point-to-Point in Ireland are not eligible for a Restricted Open race in this country. Owners must check with either the Irish Turf Club (010 353 45 41599) or the Point-to-Point Dept at the Jockey Club (071 486 4921) in which races their horses are eligible to run or subject to carry weight penalties in other categories of race.

of five years old and up that have run in National Hunt flat races in England or Ireland, or they may be early rejects from professional yards. The first mentioned animals which have run in 'Bumpers' (so-called because of their amateur jockey's supposed style of riding) are best left to cither the serious student of form or the owner of serious money. For should the horse have won his 'bumper' across the water, he will command a price which the old guard would find staggering. For example, in 1989 the winner of an Irish 'bumper' was sold at Doncaster for over £80,000. Certainly no one hoping to buy such a horse from Ireland nowadays with the intention of first racing it between the flags can expect to pay less than £20,000+ for such an animal.

As for buying a horse which has finished down the field in his 'bumper', as indicated this is best left to those who know better, as indeed is the case with any young unproven horse. The expert horseman will be an old hand at this game, and will have had plenty of experience in turning young horses round, and profiteering from them. The novice will merely find his hands overfull. As for the other type of young horse, the rejects, these are the unsuccessful or sometimes unraced animals discarded from professional yards in their annual clearout. There are many reasons why they might bc on the move. It might be because they are apparently too big and backward, or too small and too slow, or because an owner wishes to thin down his string, or has become impatient of waiting for a big horse to grow into himself, or because another owner has grown tired of waiting for his small horse to grow bigger, or they may just have proved useless under Rules. What is certain is that the potential buyer will never be told the whole truth of why the horse is being evicted.

What the buyer can and indeed must discover is whether or not the horse is sound, and this will be found out by a full veterinary examination of the horse purchaser's choice conducted by a veterinarian with specialised experience with racehorses. Many animals tendered for sale are offered with veterinary certificates at the ready. But in cases such as these it is *caveat emptor* because those examinations will have been carried out on behalf of the seller.

The reasons for caution, even when the horse comes with a warranty, is that such a guarantee is open to all sorts of interpretations by both sides. The legal implications are too complicated to be discussed here, but for interested parties the chapters entitled 'The Purchase of Horses and Veterinary

Certificates' and 'The Legal Implications of the Purchase of a Horse' in Capt. M. Horace Hayes' invaluable book *Veterinary Notes for Horse Owners* are required reading. What needs to be stressed is the importance of an examination by the intending purchaser's veterinarian, and that this report must be a written and not just a verbal one. There is, however, one more *caveat* that must be added here, with an eye on the litiginous atmosphere which seems to prevail everywhere today, and that warning cannot be expressed better than it is in Capt. Hayes' referred-to volume.

> It may be said that, because of the duty owed to a third party and the higher standard of care which a veterinarian must show, as liability exists whenever it is reasonable for one party to rely on another's skill and judgement in making a statement, a veterinarian will very rarely, if ever, warrant a horse as to soundness. This is because the definition of soundness is so wide in ambit, and because the judicial interpretation afforded the word over the years has led to the position whereby a dissatisfied party may prefer to resort to litigation as against the possibility that he or she has made a bad bargain.

Just as a chartered surveyor may be sued by his client should a report made on a property be found to be faulty, so thus may a veterinary surgeon be taken to court by the purchaser of a horse should the animal subsequently be found not to be one hundred per cent 'sound and free from vice' as might perhaps be claimed by an over-confident veterinarian. Therefore the veterinary surgeon will leave himself an escape route, and the buyer must take note of this, and thereby realise that however unblemished his prospective purchase may seem, horses are not inanimate, and cannot come fully 'guaranteed'.

The more experienced purchaser of potential point-to-point horses will be fully cognisant of this fact, as indeed he will be of the truism that no-one ever wishes to sell a good horse. But then he will also know that a very large percentage of horses racing between the flags are far from perfect, as is reflected generally by the prices paid for them, that is to say, if they belong to the normally most available type of horse, the animal which has already raced under National Hunt Rules and has either just been not quite good enough or has broken down and not mended sufficiently well to return and take the full stress of professional training. Or it may be a 'squib' from flat racing yards, a non-starter under Rules, but whose breeding lines suggest it might be happier racing over fences.

These animals are usually to be bought at the public auctions of bloodstock held at places such as Ascot and Doncaster, although the experienced buyer will get in touch with certain flat trainers when those trainers are about to have their referred-to annual clearout. These buyers, if good students of form, will probably also have seen the horses upon which they have their eyes race, and if they are sufficiently taken with the horses' pedigree as far as their jumping lines go, deals will be struck there and then rather than sending the said horses to auction. The advantage of this is that the price is pre-agreed, and there will be no chance of the prospective purchaser being carried away at the auction and finding himself paying far more than he had visualised. The disadvantage is that horses can often, at a 'cool' auction, go for a lot less at the end of a rainy afternoon in the sales ring than the often inflated prices asked for on a sunny afternoon in a swank yard. Buyers should also take care when thinking of purchasing a potential pointer from a professional trainer, since some trainers are inclined to look down their noses at point-to-point racing, and will condescendingly assure the private buyer that the horse is 'bound to win his point'.

Besides, if the selling trainer is doing his duty to his owner, he is almost honour bound to exaggerate the horse's merits. The cognoscenti know this to be the case, and therefore pay little attention to such airy confidences.

The next type of horse is the much older horse who is stepping down in class. Almost certainly an experienced handicapper with a successful record under Rules, it will make the transition to racing between the flags sometimes still under the same ownership, but more often than not it will have changed hands and its new keeper will run it in races for which it is eligible. Provided the horse is reasonably sound, it will provide excellent value for money, because as an older animal, and if a male one, almost certainly a gelding, its worth in purely financial terms will have diminished and so it will not have been an expensive purchase.

This type of horse, however, is not the most satisfactory buy for first-time owners, unless the buyers are looking for schoolmasters for their novice sons or daughters to ride. This is because the horse has most probably won under Rules and it will therefore be ineligible for certain races, and penalised in the majority of the ones for which it is admissible. Since this sort of horse is generally an older animal, it is going to be asked to carry more weight than it has ever carried in handicaps at a time of life when, if it is beginning to feel its age, it really should be carrying less. There is one more drawback to buying a ex-steeplechaser, which is that older horses earn the reputation of becoming 'thinkers', and know exactly how to look after themselves. This is of course exactly what is wanted of a schoolmaster, but prospective owners who are also ambitious may find they have bought themselves horses that do not do what is required of them by their connections, but rather what the horse decides is required of it. The horse may also find the 'softer' point-to-point fences contemptible and treat them accordingly with disdain, not jumping them properly and thus forfeiting his trump card. For under Rules it may well have won its races purely on the merit of its spectacular jumping, a major advantage round park courses but of less profitability between the flags.

It was once much more habitual for would-be owners to bid for the winners of selling races, which are contests held on occasion at National Hunt racecourses whereby the public are invited to buy at auction the winner of the 'seller' at a price 'not less than half of the advertised value' of the race. The great advantage of this particular method of purchase is that the horse will have run a very exposed trial and the prospective buyer will have gained a fairly accurate estimate of the horse's abilities. However, selling races are not what they seem, and they are full of pitfalls. If the bidding at the subsequent auction is tepid, then while it is nice to suppose that the connections have landed a nice touch and are generously stepping aside to give a new owner a chance, what is much more likely to have happened is that indeed a coup has been planned and successfully landed but with a patched up horse against extremely moderate opposition. The winner may well look as sound as a bell as he is paraded around the ring without his racing bandages for the inspection of the public, but it is not always possible to spot a 'leg' in these days of carbon implants and injections, certainly not compared with the days when the only treatment for collapsed tendons was the still controversial practice of firing, and the tell-tale scars between a fired horse's knee and fetlock told all. And if ever there was a case of *caveat emptor* it would be when offered the chance of buying the winner of a seller apparently unopposed.

On the other hand, if the amateur owner wishes to make friends and influence people, then he should on no account ever bid with any seriousness against the winning connections, who are there to buy their horse back. Contrary to what the name of the race suggests, a good horse in a selling plate is not for sale. Many a lifelong enmity has been forged after an auction where the winning connections have lost their horse either to a rival camp, or far more irritatingly, to some rookie who doesn't know the ropes. Because even if the horse goes for an inflated price, under the rules laid down for selling races the only real beneficiary is the racecourse. Finally, should the buyer ignore all these *caveats* and still be foolhardy enough to buy a winning 'plater', it should be remembered that under Rule 34 (ii) by reason of its victory that day the horse will not be eligible to run in point-to-points for a year.

Potential or proven point-to-pointers may also be bought via advertisements in *Horse and Hound, The Sporting Life*, and the regional newspapers, as well as at the smaller mixed sales whose venues and dates are advertised in the sporting press. Exactly the same procedures need to be followed when buying horses in such a way, however less formal and more 'user-friendly' may be the surroundings. In fact even more caution should be exercised, particularly when buying locally, or out of the field. It is all too easy to be swung by the friendly manner of a personable vendor, and whereas buyers have certain guarantees and comebacks if they buy through the sale rings, no such comprehensive cover is offered by the paddock dealer. The purchaser has only a dispassionate veterinary report and the evidence of his or her eyes upon which to trust, which is why when thinking of buying, play by the rules and always take a friend along, most preferably a knowledgeable one.

That disinterested pair of eyes can make all the difference. So much of the process of buying horses is emotional that the presence of an uninvolved third party is practically paramount. Faults are much more readily apparent to someone whose emotions are not involved, and even though the potential purchaser may resent the stream of criticism being directed at a horse they thought perfect, if it helps prevent the purchase of a suspect animal, the friendship will remain intact. Even if the horse passes the inspections of all concerned, a knowledgeable friend will make sure important details are not overlooked, such as what the horse has achieved previously, that it is not ineligible for the races for which it is being bought, and whether its passport is up to date and 'uncorrected'. In this last area alone, absolute vigilance is now vital, due to the Jockey Club's stringent new ruling on any alteration of a horse's vaccination details.

If the horse has run either under Rules or between the flags, its form will be there for all to see in one of the many excellent form guides (see Appendix 3). A horse which has run in handicap company will have an official handicap rating, which will give the potential purchaser a more than ready guide to its ability, and all point-to-pointers which have run, even the most moderate, will be rated in the point-to-point form books, most notably in Mackenzie and Selby's comprehensive and some would say outspoken annual, where every vice known to horse is noted, including sheep-eating. If horses could sue for libel, Messrs Mackenzie and Selby would doubtless now be selling matches on Waterloo Bridge.

When buying either at the sales or privately, the new owner must take steps to ensure the horse is covered from the moment of purchase. Both insurance and horse transport can be organised at the big sales, whereas buying privately will require a certain amount of pre-arrangement. At the sales, banking arrangements must be made in advance, and of private vendors the intending purchaser should always likewise enquire how they would like to be paid. Horses bought under warranty at the sales must be vetted within twenty-four hours and if 'spun' may be returned with no liability on the part of the purchaser. Sales catalogues always carry an explanation of the buyer's rights and liabilities, and while horses sold through the ring generally are liable to VAT, horses sold privately which are the property of unregistered persons are not. However, if in doubt, call the local Customs and Excise office. And even if a horse bought and sold privately comes without an official warranty, if it is declared by the vendor to be sound and free from vice, it may be returned whence it came if once the horse is home the buyer discovers that the animal crib bites, wind sucks, weaves, box walks or displays any other recognised and undeclared vice. But action must be taken at once, for if there is any delay in declaring the discovered vice the vendor can claim (and most often does) that the horse left his or her yard vice free, and must have picked the habit up since moving to its new home, which on the buyer's side is not always that easy to disprove.

The final category of horse is the one which as far as point-to-pointing goes, is probably the most traditional type of horse, and that is the home-bred. This makes sense when it is remembered that the first horses to go steeplechasing were hunters rather than the products of a bloodstock industry. Today's home breeder, provided he or she has the patience and the time as well as the concomitant skills, can enter into racing at grass roots level at a relatively low cost. A nice type of brood mare from a winning line, or even more preferably the dam of a National Hunt winner herself, need not be prohibitively expensive, certainly not when compared with mares purchased to breed flat racehorses. It is perfectly possible to find this sort of mare for around £2,000 to £2,500, or for half that price should she not have produced her winner. National Hunt stallions and more particularly point-to-point sires generally stand at very modest fees, ranging from £50 to £500, the average stud fee coming out at around £250. Assuming that the breeder has a few acres of paddock upon which to grow his or her equine product, and all goes well, the young horse by its fourth birthday will be eligible to run in 'bumpers', and the following year to race point-to-point. And should the horse subsequently win not only its Maiden but also a Restricted Open, let alone an Open race, besides the enormous satisfaction inherent in actually having bred a winner, the owner-breeder will have a horse worth at the very least £10,000. If exceptionally talented, it may even be sold on to a National Hunt yard for twice that amount.

This horse will of course be a thoroughbred, although under the Rules of Racing a horse whose dam is only on the Non-Thoroughbred register at Weatherbys is still eligible to race not only point-to-point but also National Hunt, hence those parenthesised items of information on steeplechase racecards which tell the racegoer that certain horses' dams are of 'pedigree untraced'. Horses whose dams are not even on the NT register may still race point-to-point, however, and the part-bred still makes many an appearance in Hunt races, and occasionally and possibly rather optimistically in the more competitive events; optimistically because however great the part-bred's courage, there is little doubt that 'an ounce of blood's worth a pound of bone'. But apart from the military, who at their meetings have races specially framed for horses which need not be registered but which have to be owned by members of the host regiment, most races are open to all, so the sporting owner-rider's best chance of gaining a success on his hunter would be to compete in one of the few 'natural country' point-to-points which still exist, or in the specially framed Heavyweight races to be found on certain racecards, rather than tackling thoroughbreds head-on.

Once novice buyers have decided on which category of horse they are to buy, there then remain several finer points to consider, which again are best thought about in the company of someone more expert, such as a friend who may also be a veterinarian, an expert amateur jockey, or simply a point-to-pointing veteran. Whichever of the experts are enrolled to help, their advice should be taken on the following matters. Firstly, they will make a recommendation as to the best age of the intended purchase, and after consideration they will most probably advise the acquisition of a middle-aged animal, an eight, nine or ten year old. Enough should be known about such a horse; even if it is still a maiden when bought, it may well have run some good races against good opposition which the expert may use as yardsticks for assessing the animal's chances over the less stiff obstacles. The horse will also be considerably cheaper if he has yet to get off the mark.

And while the animal's past form is being assessed, it is important to pay close attention to the distances over which it has been running. Until 1990 (when two and a half mile races for five, six and seven year old maidens were introduced), the minimum distance for all point-to-point races was three miles, so if a middle-aged horse which otherwise might look a likely candidate for purchase is subsequently discovered never to have run further than two miles, this should be enough to give the buyer pause for thought. For since the horse, by now say a nine year old, has never been tried over the longer distances, there must obviously have been a doubt about its stamina. If its previous trainer decided the horse was a non-stayer, and never ran it beyond two miles, then the chances are there was good reason. On the other hand, a horse who is found simply to have plodded round at the back of the field in three mile chases should also be ruled out, because point-to-point races are run at a surprisingly fast pace, and the dour stayer, unless the going is bottomless, is quite simply run off its feet.

Likewise, horses which just act in heavy going should be viewed circumspectly, since the majority of races between the flags are run on ground which is usually good, if not positively firm, particularly as the season progresses. Horses which are known mudlarks may well be in their element during the first few weeks of the season, but when it is remembered that the last point-to-point fixture is now held at the end of the first week in

June, the benefit when buying horses which act on the firm becomes readily apparent.

Size is the next consideration. There has long been a school of thought that over the jumps small horses just won't do, which basically is nonsense when you consider their track record. The Lamb, who won the Grand National in 1868 and 1871, stood barely 15 hands as a four year old, although he had grown nearly two inches by the year of his first victory. Battleship, in 1938 the winner of one of the most exciting Nationals on record, stood no more than 15.2 hands high. The extraordinary little West Country point-to-pointer Lonesome Boy, the winner (and holder of the post-war record) of 65 races, 53 of which incredibly he won in succession, as spectacular over banks as he was over fences, was a mere pony standing no more than 15 hands high. These horses are not exceptions which prove the rule, but rather they go to show that there is nothing to be said against small horses, provided they are made right and they have the heart. There is certainly no doubting their courage.

If there is a doubt about small horses it concerns their ability to carry weight. It is too much to expect a small horse to carry 12 stone 7 lb in fast run races where his unpenalised and usually larger opponents are carrying only 12 stone. Weight stops horses, and it is undeniable that it stops the smaller horses more quickly, but this is not generally the case in ladies' point-to-point races, where in races without penalties to previous winners the horses are set to carry only 11 stone. So small horses with 'toe' and an ability to jump quickly and accurately are, as they always have been, most suitable conveyances for the ladies, particularly horses which are ex-hurdlers, since animals which have shown themselves capable of jumping hurdles well and at speed but have failed to graduate to jumping steeplechase fences, generally have little trouble adapting themselves to the smaller and softer point-to-point obstacles.

Lastly, consideration has to be given to any defects which might be known about the horse. Sometimes it is possible to find these out by directly enquiring of those who may have ridden the horse professionally, unless, of course, the animal has been solely the mount of the stable jockey, whose opinion will be guarded, to say the least. If the prospective purchaser can find a jockey who may have ridden the horse as a spare ride, and who can recall the experience, the jockey might be able to remember whether or not the horse is a suitable ride for an amateur, and what its racing manners are like, i.e. does it take hold, hang, run out, jump to the left or right, take unnecessary chances, or tamely drop its bridle once the heat is on. With a bit of luck, the jockey might even have been on the horse the day the animal did itself what had been until then a previously unrevealed injury.

The veterinary examination of the intended purchase should reveal evidence of any marked defect, certainly of the legs. If the horse has at some time previously, but essentially not very recently, had tendon trouble, all need not necessarily be lost, because thanks to modern veterinary skills, provided the horse has been properly treated and then given sufficient time to heal, with further care it may race on untroubled for several seasons more. There are two points worth remembering about 'legs', however. Firstly it is never advisable to buy a horse which has not run since injuring itself, however excellent the subsequent veterinary care. It is infinitely better for the horse to have run several times since breaking down and thus have shown itself to be demonstrably sound. Secondly, horses that have 'had a leg' are said afterwards to be several pounds inferior to what they were before, perhaps as much as half a stone, maybe even more, and while this will not be the major consideration when the final decision has to be made regarding purchase, since racing point-to-point will be a step down in class for the ex-National Hunt horse, it is still worth bearing in mind when it comes to reassessing his form.

Most other major defects should be visible at examination, most particularly if a horse has had respiratory troubles and has been 'tubed', or in other words had a tracheostomy. Provided the horse has run satisfactorily since, there should be no cause for alarm, particularly since part of the required examination of the horse is to test it fully in its wind, by making the animal thoroughly exert, but not exhaust himself.* What will not show up is internal damage of the foot, and so the diligent purchaser should always request the taking of X-rays. This is not an unnecessary extravagance, but as far as racehorses are concerned is money well spent.

Backs are another source of hidden trouble, and are also worth having properly examined. Veterinarians did not always place as

* To make thoroughly certain of a horse's wind it is often considered worthwhile having the animal 'scoped', viz – the examination of the horse's breathing apparatus by an endoscope.

much importance on the condition of horses' backs as they do now, and few today will look askance if prospective purchasers request them to examine not only the horse's back but also its pelvis.

Those then are the types of horse available to the buyer, and those then are most of the accompanying *caveats*. The only other important consideration is the purpose of the whole exercise, and here it must be said that first time buyers would be well advised to look on the whole enterprise as an entertainment and not an investment. They might get lucky and find themselves owning horses which can be sold on profitably, but in the sport of racing point-to-point, this is generally unlikely. Of one thing new owners can be assured and that is they will not get rich from their winnings, the level of prize money being so miserably low; so much so that if enough people choose to celebrate, by the end of the afternoon the winning owner could well find him or herself in debit rather than in credit.

In fact the level of prize money has long been a bone of contention in the point-to-point world. The National Hunt Committee when it called the shots used the level of prize money quite cynically as a regulator, to prevent point-to-pointing from becoming a serious rival to National Hunt. And the most vociferous of point-to-pointing's supporters have always spoken out against this deliberate restriction. In 1961, when the level of prize money was finally and grudgingly increased to £40 for the winners of Opens and £30 for the winners of lesser events, John Tilling, then the Hon. Sec. of the Old Surrey and Burstow, complained bitterly, pointing out that even when this latest increase was taken into account prize money was still actually less than it had been in 1884, besides which, as other critics were quick to note, 'what they gave with one hand they took away with the other', since the Committee decreed in the same year 'that no further prize money from any source may be given'. At one stroke this ruled out the generous gifts in kind some hunts were wont to make, which in some cases included specially commissioned works of sporting art. Predictably enough, the Galloping Major Guy Cunard thought little of this, contending that point-to-point committees should be allowed to award what they could afford, disagreeing that this would disadvantage the less affluent meetings, arguing that was like saying 'Cheltenham must not put on a big race because Buckfastleigh can't match it'.

As always, however well prepared, the arguments fell on deaf ears, prize money remained at a miserable low, and the controversy went on raging. It still does, for although 1990 saw another increase, with the maximum award being raised to £250, once inflation had been accounted for prize money still stood at the same level – if not an even lower one – than it did in 1884.

TO DO OR NOT TO DO

Unlike the owners of racehorses bought to run under Rules, whose sole option (unless they be among the select few to be granted permits by the Jockey Club to train jumpers privately) is to place their animals in the yards of professional trainers, the keepers of horses destined to go point-to-pointing and/or hunter chasing have an alternative. They may send their horses to livery stables, or they may keep their horses at home and Do It Themselves.

When the sport first started this last was the rule and there were no exceptions. Pre-war owners of point-to-pointers were usually landed folk of one complexion or another, either farming, military or estate owning families, whose roots had always been in the land, and whose interest in and affection for horses stemmed from hunting. They kept their horses at home, and the animals were produced for hunting and racing by specially delegated staff. Training yards were unheard of, because there was simply no need of them.

This attitude still holds good in some of the more distant areas even today, where the professional livery yard is all but unknown. In the whole of the Northern Area, for instance, it appears that there is only one such establishment, since the majority of the area's point-to-pointers are qualified, trained and usually ridden by the same people, namely their owners. Livery yards are still regarded as improperly 'professional', and will not be seen as necessary until the 'accountants, solicitors, and builders etc, from Edinburgh, Carlisle and Newcastle can be persuaded that point-to-pointing is fun and that they don't have to own acres of land to take part'.

This fact was discovered many years ago in the Midlands and the South, initially just after the war when, as has already been indicated, people from more ordinary backgrounds began to buy horses capable of racing point-to-point for their teenage children

who had enjoyed following hounds, usually with their local Pony Club, and now wanted to have some fun racing between the flags. This new type of owner usually came from more straightened circumstances, and could afford the purchase and keep of a point-to-pointer only if the family qualified and trained the animal themselves.

It was very much make-and-do, and in many cases it still is even nowadays. An old outhouse, cow-byre or barn was converted into a form of loosebox, and training facilities had to be improvised, depending on where the family lived. If they were near downland then they could count their blessings and never have to worry about where to gallop their horse. On the other hand, if there was no good common grassland in their vicinity, they would have to rely on the goodwill of their local farmer, since they would need to seek his permission to work their horse round the edge of his fields. The family would perhaps take it in turns to ride 'work', or else each one would be assigned a task in the training rota, feeding, mucking out, grooming and exercise. Which are the self-same tasks the modern owner faces should he choose to Do It Himself.

The great advantage of training from home is the total involvement. Anyone who has produced a horse fit enough just to run and finish in a point-to-point, let alone get placed in or even win one, speaks enthusiastically of the experience, for to the real racing enthusiast there is nothing to match the euphoria engendered by the thrill of watching a home-trained, home-fed, and often home-bred horse come home. Even those who have previously owned winners of good races under Rules and later on have taken up point-to-pointing for that famous bit of 'fun' are unable to compare the two experiences, having found to their eternal stupefaction greater satisfaction in saddling the winner of their Members' Race at Larkhill than in being the owner of one 'leg' of a horse professionally trained to win one or two moderate handicap hurdles.

The disadvantage of training from home is the total involvement. What began as a sideline fast becomes an obsession. Thoroughbred horses in training are totally demanding creatures, and cannot be neglected or ignored for a moment. Moreover, they are creatures of habit, and the name of the habit is routine. For the home trainer there will be no more winter dawns spent lying in bed. He or she will be up and about mucking out and feeding often long before the dawn chorus has even begun

Opposite: 'East west, home's best', and the same goes for training winners. Whit-sunday, one of the nicest debutants of the 1990 season is produced by his 'family', with whom he is seen return-ing to the winner's enclosure at Larkhill, with Mark Chamberlayne up. (Sporting Life)

warming up, for horses run to a timetable, which must be followed religiously. A late meal, or a canter given mid-afternoon rather than early morning may well upset a horse, and lead to a sulk or worse, an unfinished meal. Children thrive on routine because it gives them security, and horses are no different. An ill observed timetable, or worse, a slap-happy training procedure, with mucking out done whenever possible rather than whenever necessary, feeds hastily prepared and thrown into the horse's manger at uncertain times, and exercise given with regard to the convenience of the owner rather than the need of the horse, can lead to a horse becoming fretful, and as yet no one is altogether certain of quite how many stable vices are born out of such anxieties.

Any professional yard will underwrite the value of a good staff, all of whom will have been taught the value of a strictly observed daily procedure. The owner-trainer then would do well to follow suit to the best of his ability. Given the ideal family circumstances, with both parents and children keen to help, then most of the onerous tasks can be done before it is time for various members of the team to go to work or college, leaving the person holding the fort the less arduous tasks, such as feeding and routine surveillance.

Above and right: Everything a livery yard should be. Caroline Saunder's successful outfit in the Midlands, cheerful, efficient and friendly. (Trevor Meeks)

What attracts the novice owner to the idea of training at home is that provided sufficient facilities are at hand, the job requires less applied equestrianism than other competitive horse sports, such as eventing. The diligent eventer is required to face more disciplines by the nature of the chosen recreation, and will need to 'practise' more, particularly the horse's groundwork. A racehorse also needs to be worked, but the work is usually much more simple, and provided the horse is not an out and out lunatic (in which case he has no business in the yard of the rookie trainer) then his basic exercise, on roads and hills, can be managed by any competent member of the family. If one of the family is also to ride the horse racing, then his fast work and his schooling can also be undertaken 'in house'.

As has been said, much depends on what facilities lie to hand. But when and if they do not, one of the most heartening aspects of the sport is the co-operative nature of most of its contestants. Therefore beginners should never be afraid to ask for help and advice, and they will be astonished by the amount of assistance they will be offered by those they perhaps viewed only as potential rivals. When circumstances permit neighbouring owner-trainers may well offer the use of their gallops and schooling fences, the only proviso probably being that any damage inflicted on their precious jumps will be repaired at the exerciser's expense. Very soon the novice owner-trainer may well be riding out with and working his or her horses against a neighbouring string, an advantage which cannot be valued too highly. For one of the drawbacks of training at home is the lack of competition on the gallops. Too often small private trainers find that they have nothing against which to work their horses in the final stages of their training, a factor which is particularly disadvantageous if their animals are young and inexperienced, and need to be worked in company.

Sometimes it is possible to establish a good working relationship with the local livery yard, which will sometimes enable privately owned horses to be worked with a big string, an advantage which if accorded will help the education of any young horse enormously. Whether or not such a favour is granted, private trainers should make every effort to establish as many useful contacts as possible with other owner-trainers so that they may ride work together. Or if they live near an area such as Larkhill, they will find for the price of an annual permit they will be allowed to gallop their horses at certain permitted times within the boundaries but not actually upon the racecourse proper. Schooling of horses, that is over the jumps, is not allowed on any course until 'after the final meeting has been held, and permission has been obtained from the land-owner concerned, and the clerk of the course of the host hunt in whose country the point-to-point meeting is held.'*

Given that novice owner-trainers have suitable stabling, acceptable facilities and co-operative families, their greatest shortcoming will be a lack of experience. Even if their small family yard has been turning out their hunters successfully for several seasons, there is a world of difference between getting and then keeping a half or three-quarter bred hunter fit, which is difficult enough, and the successful production of thoroughbred racehorses. As with most things, it is finally a case of trial and error, but since the trainer's subject matter is animate rather than inanimate, the lessons learned through the making of errors should preferably be academic ones. The appointment of the best recommended farrier in the area, and the regular attendance likewise of the best racing veterinarian will help forestall the making of any major injudicious and potentially

* Note C7, JC regulations for P/P steeplechases.

injurious gaffes, as will the solicitation of the best advice. Too many people are too proud to ask for help when they most need it, considering that they will be privately mocked, but in fact the very reverse is the case. Novices who refuse to benefit through the experience of others will not appear in the eyes of their critics to be behaving with undue modesty but rather will seem to be playing the know-it-all, and consequently may be ridiculed. The willingness of people to help and to share their knowledge of the sport with the initiate simply cannot be stressed enough.

The disadvantage of inexperience can also be greatly mollified, if the pockets of the new owner-trainer are deep enough, by the employment of a good groom. The larger established private yards by necessity all employ professional help, as do many of the two to three horse set-ups. And there is absolutely no doubt at all as to the all round benefit gained. However, since the employment of a groom is in importance second only to the purchase of the stable's potential point-to-pointer, the most careful consideration should be given at the time of selection. Again, horses are very like children in that they are much inclined to take their tones from their governors. Horses that get shouted at, slapped around the head and pushed about in their box with pitchforks soon reflect the manners of their bad tempered keepers. Ask any wise equestrian and they will tell you there are no such things as bad horses, only bad people.

The actual technique of training the horse merits a book to itself, and there are many excellent publications on the market, a selection of which may be found in Appendix 7, which will guide and instruct apprentice home trainers. In the years to come no doubt particular and personal methods will be refined, but all good training techniques should be founded on the advice of those more experienced. The only two points to deal with here both concern responsibility, one to the rider, and the other to the horse. Firstly, whoever trainers intend to put up on their horses, they owe it to the jockeys to make sure they have done their level best to educate their horses properly. There are many cheerful and optimistic souls about who believe that provided they stuff enough corn into their animals and give them a stiff gallop before racing that they have done their job. They will not have bothered to school their intended runner over regulation fences, since because it jumped anything and everything when it was being qualified, the owners assume a few forgiving birch hedges will not pose it any great problems. This is not the case, and good jockeys dread having to ride such horses. Three miles and eighteen fences taken at racing pace are very different from a three mile point out hunting, taken at a moderate gallop with the chance of taking several good pulls, if not the odd check.

Horses trained in this haphazard way often will arrive at the races with no appointed pilot. The inexperienced jockey, on the look-out for a spare ride, will get talked into riding animals which anyone in their right senses would do well to refuse. The experienced jockey knows that the good horses are spoken for, and the rides on them will only come up for grabs should their regular pilots be sidelined through injury. He or she will avoid at all costs the chance to ride any animal presented in the parade ring with its paddock sheet half off, lathered in sweat and a couple of helpers trying to hold its head.

Likewise, the responsibility owner-trainers bear towards their horses is of no less import. There is always a danger of running horses too frequently point-to-point, the dictum being that while they are sound and they are eating up and the going is right for them, no harm will be done. The temptation is much greater for private trainers who might have only one or two horses in their yards. Loving the sport the way they do, and seeing a clean manger the day after their horse has last raced, they will be more than inclined to give it another outing within the fortnight, if not indeed the following weekend. Horses are expected to run fortnightly between the flags, and if the horse in question can only act in the soft, then provided he is one hundred per cent sound there is an argument to be made for running him that frequently early on, since he will not be suited by conditions later in the season. There is also an argument to be made for running sound point-to-pointers with this much greater frequency if comparison is made with National Hunt racing in Ireland, where fit horses often compete bi-weekly. Proponents of this approach argue that the reason National Hunt yards in this country do not run the horses in their charge so often is that the size of their strings make this an inconvenience, which it is claimed has led to the perpetuation of a myth which declares that a horse needs at least a month between races. What is forgotten is that when and where horses are raced more intensely, subsequently and invariably there is a much higher rate of breakdown. Public trainers with other people's valuable horses in their care feel it their duty to adopt a more conservative approach, while small private point-to-point trainers with only a couple of their own horses to produce are less prudent, and all too easily and sometimes perhaps even wilfully dismiss the tell-tale signs of their horses' growing weariness or indeed of their imminent unsoundness.

Therefore it is recommended that novice trainers should err on the side of caution rather than recklessness. There is relatively little to be gained by the over-frequent racing of a horse. Youngsters may well become quickly disenchanted and older horses bored. The chances of owner-trainers getting the two or three horses in their respective stables through the season without damage shorten with every run, particularly once the going firms up and the state of many courses deteriorates, so if in doubt, wait.

A large percentage of the people most recently attracted to the sport have come from very untraditional backgrounds. They usually have little or no connection with hunting, although some may take up following hounds as a weekend amusement, nor are they regular inhabitants of the countryside. Instead this new breed of owner is drawn from the towns, and the cities, and is attracted to point-to-pointing as a way of being able to race a horse without incurring the astronomic costs associated with buying and running a steeplechaser under Rules. But since this new type of owner is basically a town dweller, they have nowhere of their own to stand their horses, and so they turn to the livery yards.

Previous to this, livery yards had existed in the country mainly for the housing and supply of riding horses, and hirelings for hunting. They were as their name described, with no pretensions at being anything else. These yards were now being asked to stand point-to-pointers at livery, in order that the horses might be regularly and fairly hunted and thus qualify for the necessary Hunters' Certificates. Within this request, however, lay a tacit agreement that the proprietor should also prepare these horses for the point-to-point season, in other words, to train them. But under the rules of racing point-to-point, horses which stood in 'professional' trainers' yards were ineligible to race, so therefore those who had been delegated to look after a third party's horses with the intention of getting the animals ready to race between the flags must not be called trainers. Instead they were still to be known as the proprietors of livery yards, regardless of the fact that the purpose of their establishments was now to train horses to race point-to-point. However, this seemed to satisfy the racing authorities, who had learned a long time ago that the sporting of blinkers need not necessarily be confined to horses.

To compound this anomaly, even though an ever increasing number of horses came to be trained in these livery yards, it was ruled that the name of the owner was always to be given as that of the trainer, regardless of where the horse was standing. This was very confusing to the general public, particularly to those not so well versed in the refinements of the sport. It was also very unfair, since only the expert student of form could possibly know which horses were being trained and run from home, and which had been sent out from one of the powerful livery yards. And as that self-same expert student of form would be the first to confess, there is usually a world of difference between the horses turned out from the big livery yards and those done in someone's back yard.

Now, mainly thanks to the concerted efforts of Messrs Mackenzie and Selby who have long campaigned for a distinction to be made between the two types of trained horse, it is possible to find out who 'trains' what and where. But this information is still not to be found on the racecard, nor in the results columns of *The Sporting Life* and *Horse and Hound*. The only information printed there still is the name of the owner and the qualifying hunt. The required information is only to be found in *The Racing Post Record*, edited by the aforenamed Messrs Mackenzie and Selby. But it must be noted this excellent publication is a record of the results of races run the previous season, and thus can only be used with hindsight and as a guide for horses that have run before, and which to the best of the compilers' knowledge have not changed stables, or rather livery yards. The famous 'average punter' is just as much in the dark as he always was, as to who actually trains the horse of his choice, and it is only through perhaps observing who is saddling the animal up that the punter might have the slightest idea who has produced the horse, and then only provided he is visually conversant with all the livery yard proprietors, and the owner-trainers, or has read the skimpy pre-race information in one of the few daily papers which afford the sport any coverage. Paddock-spotting, however, can be additionally fraught with danger for the average racegoer, because due to the camaraderie that generally exists within the sport well-known livery yard owners when they have no runner themselves are often to be found giving an owner-trainer chum a helping hand in the parade ring. It therefore pays the serious student of point-to-pointing to study not only the form of the horses but also that of the connections.

Once the ground rules came to be understood, there was a rapid proliferation of livery yards, most particularly, as noted, in the south of England. Some developed from the yards of farming families who had long been involved with racing between the flags, the owners either building some more loose boxes, but more often than not simply converting existing and unwanted farm buildings into stables capable of housing the ever increasing flow of horses. Others, yards already in the business of keeping horses professionally, either expanded their enterprise or replaced their hirelings with more and more point-to-pointers. Both of these types of yards grew organically, which is to say they were the natural result of a ready and growing demand.

Other yards were created perhaps more deliberately, custom-built with an eye on accommodating the needs of the new type of owner. These premises might previously have been the site of successful and expertly run event yards, or they might have belonged to farmers who had seen more future and certainly more fun in training point-to-pointers than in continuing to try and earn a living under the umbrella of the Common Market. Whatever the reason for their 'conversion', the yards which have grown and prospered are the ones run by proprietors rich in equestrian experience, 'guv'nors' who have either ridden point-to-point since they were legally allowed, or who have spent their professional life producing competition horses. Prime examples of these different but equally excellent kinds of stables are John Dufosee's tremendously successful yard in the West Country, and Miss Henrietta Knight's model but much more formal establishment (before she took out a licence to train under Rules) in Oxfordshire.

Once the decision has been made to place their horses in a livery yard, new owners have to decide which one. Were they putting a horse with a professional trainer to go National Hunt racing, they would more likely be swayed by the reputation of the trainer first and the location of the said yard second, because public trainers send their horses greater distances to race, and most owners of horses racing under Rules do not wish the same sense of involvement that the owners of point-to-pointers do. For the latter, there is a great attraction in having the livery yard of their choice on their door step; not just so that they can chew the cud with the proprietor, but also because point-to-point racing is very much a local activity, and horses by and large are raced within a much smaller radius, on average one of about sixty or seventy miles. The more powerful yards will travel further on occasion, John Dufosee frequently making the trip from Dorset to Cambridge and beyond, while Caroline Saunders mounts many a raid on the south eastern and western areas from her highly successful Midlands base.

Even so, any new owner's choice of livery yard will be governed by its proximity first and foremost, particularly as they will most probably wish to enjoy the sense of involvement so peculiar to point-to-pointing. Good yards will encourage this, but new owners should make quite sure of their welcome before committing their horses to anyone's care. Many a first time racehorse owner has been wooed with a skilfully designed cocktail of bonhomie and whisky, only to find that once they have actually placed their horse in the yard the doors are then shut to them. With livery yards, this is most certainly not the general rule, but nonetheless, new owners should always make sure they and their prospective trainer are mutually sympathetic.

What the various livery yard proprietors are like may be discovered on the grapevine or by diligent interviewing. Owners should always take into account trainers' racing records, because however charming and convincing the trainer may appear to be, owners will be paying around the same amount of money for their horses to stand in unsuccessful yards as in successful ones. First time owners need not be deterred, however, on their visit of initial inspection by the often apparent delapidation of the yard buildings. Not if a closer examination reveals the seemingly shabby boxes to be warm and relatively draught-proof, with deep clean beds, supple and clean tack, horses well groomed, fit and fed, and above all a happy atmosphere prevailing in the yard. If such is the case owners can be assured the proprietor has his priorities in the right order. Point-to-pointing is not a rich and glamorous sport, but then neither is it an absurdly expensive one. So better the yard that is more concerned with its horses than with its cosmetics.

For the first time owner who lives outside the designated area, the people to ask as to where the livery yards lie are the Hunt Secretary, and the Hunt's Point-to-Point Secretary, who are not one and the same person. One or both of them will provide the necessary information. The Point-to-Point Owners' Association, which any newcomer would do well to join (see Appendix 8), will also give advice and help freely, as will the Area Secretary, any member of the local hunt's point-to-point committee, and other 'qualifiers'. Enquiries will need to be made, because the big livery yards never advertise, simply because they do not need to do so. Small yards advertise, but these should perhaps be viewed somewhat cautiously, as many of them are private yards with two or three point-to-pointers of their own, who just wish to help finance the racing of their small string by attracting one or two paying guests.

The reason why this may not be a good idea let alone the best one is that the private yard will inevitably put its own horses first, however altruistic it tries to be. This is particularly true of stables run by those who also ride their horses point-to-point, since it is practically impossible not to favour the home horses when the time comes to make the decision as to who runs where and when. The paying guest may therefore well be sidelined until the following meeting not because it isn't fit, but because the owner of the yard wants his own horses to stand the best chance. So new owners who are subscribers to the small is beautiful notion, would perhaps be best advised to choose a yard which is run from the ground and not from the racing saddle.

If they do elect to go to a small private yard, then it should be a small yard with a record of successes, and even more preferably one whose wins have not all been gained by just one horse, particularly a 'grand old steeplechaser' who won a string of races under Rules, and is now giving his owners a bit of local sport without them having to do too much training. There are, however, some excellent yards to be found, run usually by 'professional' amateurs, in other words, families who have been doing it themselves for years and sometimes even generations. What they do not know about horses is not usually worth knowing, but entry into such yards is not always easy, since by and large these people prefer to concentrate on 'family' horses. Some other smaller yards who have had their first winners are quite deliberately expanding, and trying to attract outside custom, and new owners may sometimes strike lucky with them, but usually only if a rule of thumb is followed, namely that the horses standing in the yard in outside ownership should outnumber the horses standing in the possession of the proprietors.

Whichever sort of livery yard is chosen, big, small, professional or amateur, if it is a good yard then new owners will have their hands held from start to finish. The types of races will be explained to them, as will the responsibilities they themselves will have to shoulder. They will also be told, should they not have enquired already, what extra costs they will be in for, and these may well include, depending on the stables, shoeing, veterinary charges, and all medical care called in from the outside, entries, transport, gallops, wormers, and postage. As far as entries go, owners are generally asked to sign a batch of blank entry forms at the beginning of the season, although where and when their horses are finally to run will be discussed and decided mutually nearer the date. The good stable will supply all the tack, exercise and travel rugs, paddock sheets and blankets, although extra stable wear (rugs and blankets) is always welcome. The good trainer will answer all the owners' questions, however naïve, which is why it is well to choose someone of unlimited patience, or at least someone whose other half possesses that redoubtable virtue. If they so wish, owners can see their horses being schooled, cantered and galloped. If they are themselves keen riders, they may be invited to ride out in the mornings. If they are as competent as they are willing, they may even be invited to ride work. Trainers are usually short of good work riders, and good riders are more than welcome. But before they volunteer their services on the gallops, however enthusiastic the owners may be, they should obtain a verdict on their work-riding capabilities from an unbiased third party. Being 'carted' on the gallops when the guv'nor has given the jockey strict orders to drop in behind is never the most salutary of experiences.

In return for all this, first time owners will also be expected to do their fair share of listening, particularly when it comes to the placing and running of their horses. Because it is not just a question of where and when, but with a young horse or a horse of unknown quantity more a question of how. This is one of the hardest aspects of racehorse ownership, learning how to stand by and how to interpret the signals. Because even though owners may feel their involvement to be total, the one thing they will not quite be told is the whole truth about their horse. Half the reason for this is that often the trainer and the jockey do not actually know it themselves. The other half of the reason is that when they do know owners are generally going to be the last people they tell.

There are various reasons for this. Firstly sensible trainers do not like to be found out. Not for them the prophet-like announcements others less circumspect are prone to make on the gallops after an impressive piece of work. Nor will they pronounce after the horse's first race, however promising, that the animal will win next time out. The good and sensible trainers are too wise and canny for this, probably due to the fact that in their salad days they were more than once caught out making predictions, only for the horses to go down with a bundle of owners' money on it. Secondly, wise and experienced trainers know that as much as they may think they know, there is always something more to be learned. Time and time again they may have seen what they think to be potentially brilliant horses run blinders first or second time out, only to find that when the heat is really on the horses either do not see the trip out or simply will not. So they hold their cards close to their chests, however excited they may be inside at their horses' prospects.

They will also keep their opinions to themselves if they are any good at business, for should any of the horses in their care show signs of being 'plugs' they may well reason that is for their owners to find out, and so it is at times like these that novice owners should learn how to read the signs. If they have no real eye for reading their horses' ability on the gallops or during a race, then their only hope is to learn how to decode the crypticisms which pepper the post-mortems held post-gallop and race. Some trainer-isms are included in the glossary at the back of the book.

Owners must also learn the difference between a horse being pulled up and a horse being 'pulled up'. A horse is normally pulled up when it has lost all chance of featuring in the outcome of the race. Others are pulled up if they have hurt themselves, made a noise, or burst a blood vessel. Young horses, however, may also be pulled up when it is considered that they have done quite enough in the race, particularly if it is the animal's first time out. This could well account for the apoplectic facial hue sported by many of the stewards, who know perfectly well that they are witnessing a forbidden act, namely the schooling of a horse in public, but are powerless to do anything about it if the horse appears to have dropped himself out of the race, usually and conveniently on the far side of the course. Some horses are, however, resistant to being pulled, and despite their pilot's efforts to haul them up, take hold and charge home, showing all and sundry quite how potentially brilliant they are, earning the unfortunate pilot a private wigging in the car park for not stopping the animal once it had got the idea.

Other pilots even less fortunate have been known to pull their horses up right under the stewards' noses when leading by a distance and having their arms pulled out. One jockey to be caught in such a fashion, when hauled up in front of the Stewards at Tweseldown in the 1989 season, offered as his excuse for pulling the horse up the fact that he was afraid he might fall at the next fence. The Stewards were neither convinced nor amused and promptly asked the young man for a cheque for £200.

Once they have established a relationship with their trainer, new owners will soon learn the ropes, particularly if they are the sort of people who learn by watching. For they will find one of the main advantages of having a horse in a livery yard is that they will be able to draw comparisons, particularly should the owner choose to stay for a mug of tea the morning the stable's string has been given its final work-out before a forthcoming race and listen to what the work-riders and jockeys have to say. In the banter of these traditional sessions around the proprietor's kitchen table the relative merits and prospective chances of the stable's horses are discussed, and the attentive owner will learn how well or how disappointingly each horse has worked. Gallops are hard to 'read', especially for the non-rider, so anything the jockey has to say about the way the owner's horse has just worked should be well marked and properly digested. Many an owner is often under the impression that his or her horse has just galloped rather impressively, only to be told by the pilot that the animal was off the bridle and struggling to hold its place for the last half a furlong. Or conversely one week later when the same horse appeared to be idling and looking about it, the owner might learn during another breakfast post-mortem that the jockey was holding the horse up and that it could have picked off the horses in front at any time.

Even if the owner's horse is not entered at the next meeting, it is almost certain that one or two of the others from the stable will have been. And if they are horses which have worked alongside the owner's, then the races which they subsequently run should prove highly instructive, as should the trainer's assessment of their performances. One thing new owners must assuredly learn at these times, however, is that if the meaning of what is being said is not clear, then they must ask for amplification. Too often owners are afraid to ask why, for fear of betraying their ignorance, which is wrong, because the real ignorance actually lies in not enquiring.

This is a point which cannot be stressed enough, and is underwritten by the advice solicited from those right at the top of the sport.

'The only suggestion to a new entrant to the sport is to seek the best advice. There are plenty of experienced folk who would be delighted to advise if asked but are too modest to offer.'

(Charles Sample)

'For those literally starting from scratch, go to their local meetings and watch, look, listen and learn. The efficient people will evolve. ASK for help. It is amazing how helpful people are, especially if they realise the potential participant is prepared to learn and work at the sport. They will willingly part with their knowledge, acquired over many years, and learned through their own mistakes.'

(John Dufosee)

'I think the most important thing for any newcomer to point-to-pointing is always to remember that it should be fun, and an enjoyable day out for everyone involved, including relations, friends and supporters. I try to encourage my owners to come and see their horses work and school and therefore get to know the staff and the team behind the scenes. I try to help my owner-riders as much as possible to improve themselves and their horses as there is nothing like success to encourage further participation.

One other piece of advice I would also give to a newcomer to the sport is never to be afraid to ask for help. There are always people ready and willing to assist anyone, either to walk the course, saddle up or just give moral support. We are so very lucky to be involved in a sport where we can meet so many friendly people, all of whom have the enthusiasm to turn up year in, year out to give their vital assistance in running a point-to-point.'

(Caroline Saunders)

'WILD, MAD RIDERS'

'I know of no worse sight than seeing those enormous men, many with turnip heads and oversize bodies, dressed in ill-fitting clothes from some lease-lend tailor which fit only where they touch, bumping round like half-trained mounted policemen on some wretched animals, with whips stinging off them for the last mile and no chance of finishing anywhere!'

Thus wrote a Lambourn trainer, one Capt. Sandy Carlos Clarke, in the correspondence columns of *The Sporting Life* in 1961, precipitating a long-continued controversy as to the merits or demerits (as the Captain saw them) of contemporary point-to-point jockeys. It was an ill-judged outburst, and led many to call for a public apology to what their spokesman described as 'one of the greatest band of sportsmen in the world'. Michael Williams, who recounts the incident in his book on point-to-pointing, takes great delight in 'adding to Capt. Carlos Clarke's discomfiture' by listing some of the 'turnip-heads' then riding point-to-point and so publicly disparaged by the choleric Captain, a register which included Guy Cunard, Bob McCreery, Gay Kindersley, Ian Balding, John Lawrence (now Lord Oaksey), Michael Tory, Peter Brookshaw, Edward Cazalet, Sir William Pigott-Brown, and a young man who was to be the joint champion National Hunt jockey only seven years later, Bob Davies.

It was probably the most outspoken attack on the participants of the sport since the days of Nimrod and Surtees, although to be sure there had always been a school of thought which reckoned the majority of point-to-point riders to be unworthy of proper consideration. Some of these critics' descendants still go racing, and are regularly to be heard holding forth about the standard of riding, particularly after Ladies' races. But then even if the ladies rode as well as the likes of Peter Scudamore and Richard Dunwoody they would win no praise from these grandstand

No turnip-heads here. The Men's Open at the Army point-to-point, Tweseldown, 1989. The stylish rider extreme right is Simon Claisse, the sport's new 'man' at Portman Square. (John Beasley)

criticasters, who are of the complexion that wherever a woman's place might be, it is most certainly not on the back of a racehorse.

Fortunately the average point-to-point enthusiast is a more well-informed and enlightened person, appreciative of both the skill and the courage of both species of jockey. Anyone with a proper understanding of the sport knows that because it is a purely amateur one, the jockeys are bound to come in all shapes and sizes, since the game is their hobby, not their way of life. Those who ride professionally often do so because they are of a particular height and weight. But for the people who ride point-to-point their jobs are first and their hobby second.

And since those who race-ride between the flags come from all walks of life, it is hardly surprising that visually they do not appear a uniform bunch. The names chalked up on the racecourse number-board belong to deep-sea divers, grain merchants, brick layers, commodity brokers, trainer's sons and daughters, writers, coal miners, insurance agents, the offspring of both tenant and gentlemen farmers, chartered surveyors, students, soldiers, mothers, lawyers, farmworkers, doctors, bookmakers, housewives, lords and secondhand car salesmen, and it would be difficult to imagine a more disparate bunch than that. It would be long odds indeed on their mothers or nannies informing any of them at an early age that their futures lay only in race-riding.

The framing of the weights to be carried in point-to-point races reflects the type of jockey attracted by the sport. Leaving aside hunter chases for the moment, ladies are expected to carry a minimum of 11 stone, and men rarely less than 12*. There has always been plenty of contention as to what constitutes a fair weight for horses to carry racing between the flags, one side arguing that 12 stone is too much for a horse to carry three miles, young or old, and that 12½ stone is verging on the cruel. This side proposes that in Mens' and Mixed races the maximum unpenalised weight should be 11½ stone, and 10½ for Ladies', while their opponents counter by arguing that for amateurs, 12 stone is a 'makeable' weight, and allows the average fit horseman of a certain age to participate in the game he loves, without having to sweat it off, or poison himself with diuretics. Certainly the tallest of today's jockeys, some of whom are well over six foot, would find it very difficult to make 11½ stone. But then many of the competing horses in their turn find the burden of carrying 12½ stone over three and sometimes four miles too much for them in turn to 'do'.

Whatever the rights or wrongs of this argument, it would be an undeniable shame if some of the game's bigger and taller pilots were weighted out. Even so, it is perhaps worth re-considering the weights horses should carry over the maximum distance races, whatever their previous achievements. One hundred and seventy-five pounds over seven thousand and forty yards and twenty-five four-and-a-half foot fences is an almost intolerable burden, whatever the size of the horse. There is certainly a case for making these protracted races either non-penalty affairs, or to start the weights lower as suggested, at

Opposite, above: No marks lost for style here either. The ladies in full cry at the Staff College point-to-point, Tweseldown 1968. (Frank H. Meads)

Opposite, below: Tinker, tailor, soldier, sailor? No, from front to back, head girl, grain broker, deep-sea diver, bloodstock shipping agent, farmer, bookmaker, and university student. The many faces of the sport's jockeys. (Kit Houghton)

---

* The exceptions being when riding 5yo (allowed 7lb) and mares of 6yo and upwards (allowed 5lb).

11½ stone. After all, a four mile race is a true test of stamina and really needs little else in the way of further embellishment.

Likewise there may well be a case to be argued that, as in professional racing, those classed as beginners should be entitled to a riding allowance, of say seven pounds, until such time as they have ridden half a dozen winners. Anyone, however potentially talented, is surely entitled to receive some sort of weight concession from their highly experienced rivals while they are still learning the ropes. There are, it has to be admitted, some races framed especially for young riders who have not won more than a certain amount of races, but these are few and very far between.

The radical elements will even go so far as to suggest that when ladies ride against the men, they should be entitled to claim. Not all the lady jockeys would agree with this, however, since many of them consider themselves good enough to take the opposite sex on at level weights and beat them, as did their adventurous predecessors, but it is almost certain that the less experienced girls, the ones riding in their first mixed races, would be grateful for an allowance. What the men might think

Not many men would want ladies as good as the once again hatless Miss Covell claiming weight in mixed races, here seen winning the Ladies' at Edenbridge in 1952. (John Topham Ltd)

of it would in the main probably be unprintable, since there are a considerable number of male jockeys still greatly opposed to the notion of unisex racing. This disputatious subject will be returned to later, but suffice it to say here that there are more than a few male jockeys who would actually prefer the female of the species to be made to carry more weight, not less, for the privilege of racing against them. Point-to-pointing may be a very friendly sport, but it is also a very hotly contested one.

Most riders graduate to the sport in a fairly orthodox and predictable way, namely through the Pony Club and then the hunting field. Pony clubs, formed by hunts to encourage and harness the potential of the rapidly increasing numbers of children who had taken to keeping and riding ponies after the Second World War, were the seed bed. Their instruction was of the highest quality, and their pupils were taught not only to improve the riding and care of their ponies, but were introduced to fairly intensive competition, much of which took place cross-country.

The natural graduation was of course to the hunting field, where the growing child, particularly the adventurous one, tasted the heady thrills of galloping fast in company over lines of hedges and ditches. It was then only a matter of time before the child, now grown to teenage, was attracted to having a go over the point-to-point fences, and parents were then solicited to purchase a suitable conveyance. If the family was united in its purpose, then buying a horse was the only way to get its offspring started, because unless the teenager had shown some quite exceptional talent, for instance at one day eventing, or perhaps junior team-chasing, then it would be highly unlikely that any rational outsider would offer a totally inexperienced novice the ride on an even half-way decent horse.

So ideally the new recruit would gain experience on custom-bought schoolmasters in their Members' Races, and contests reserved for young riders. Encouraged they might perhaps cut a few more teeth riding in Adjacents and Restricted Opens, rather than Maidens, which are often, just like Novice Chases under Rules, the most grief-stricken of races in which to ride. Much depends on the eligibility of the horses which have been bought for the debutants. If the animal is an ex-winning handicapper, then it will be ineligible for Maidens anyway, and penalised to the maximum in most other contests. This will be of no consequence to either the rider or the connections, since the

Young horses need all the schooling they can get, as witnessed here by Michael Felton doing his best to get Trust The Gypsy out of his habit of falling.
(Kit Houghton)

purpose of the exercise is most probably simply to educate the jockey.

Those connections already steeped in the game will perhaps have sent their jockeys to 'school' before introducing them to the racecourse proper. They will have asked a friend or acquaintance, preferably one still riding competitively, to teach their offspring the rudiments of race-riding, and educate them in the art of jumping birch at racing pace. Then, to complete the initial part of the apprentice's tuition, if the parents enjoy a good relationship with their local livery yard, the proprietor might be persuaded to let the novice ride gallops, and possibly even school his or her horse over the stable's practice jumps. Certainly the thinking family will wish to pack as much pre-race experience into their jockey as is humanly possible.

Not everyone of course makes the transition from pony clubs to race-riding, although it should be mentioned here in case of any misunderstanding, that the Pony Club as such do not actively encourage any link between its own activities and riding point-to-point. They do emphasise the hunting connection, and even nowadays polo no less, but oddly enough they leave their young members to find their own way to the racecourse. Those with no Pony Club connection whatsoever come to the sport again either through hunting, or an associated equestrian activity, such as eventing, or they might be the sons or daughters of professional trainers who have grown up in a racing environment, riding work and schooling since they were old and strong enough to do so. Many a trainer's child is to be found riding point-to-point, often with little if any previous hunting experience. They are sometimes advantaged by the fact that their parents have been given gift horses by owners, animals which are perhaps considered too old or infirm to continue their careers under Rules, but still willing and able enough to teach youngsters the art of getting safely round the race-track.

Would-be jockeys need not necessarily be good orthodox horsemen. In fact there are examples to be found of people in their twenties, thirties, and even their forties taking up racing point-to-point without any previous riding experience whatsoever. The quintessential race-rider is not at all the most knowledgeable equestrian. He or she will be a person with the best balance, most suitable physique, the greatest ability to see a 'stride', the most sensitive hands, and the greatest ability to apply his or her intelligence. There is no doubt at all that if the initiate has been brought up on a horse and gained experience hunting and success riding competitively, then the art of riding racehorses is going to prove a lot more accessible than it is to the complete novice who walks into an instructor's yard having only previously sat on a seaside donkey. Nonetheless, starting from scratch is not an impossibility, is frequently done, and not always by those in the first flush of youth.

A study of the illustrations should provide a fair example of how much the style of riding point-to-point has changed, and never more so than since the mid-1960s. Television has played a crucial role in refining the way amateurs ride, since before televised racing very few youngsters were committed racegoers, and so consequently the only riders they could try and emulate were those they saw at their local tracks racing between the flags. And those riders themselves, unless they were steeplechasing fanatics, or born into racing families, more or less inherited their style from their forebears who rode their races in much the same way as they followed hounds, upright with a good long length of leather. Some, as the photograph on page 110 shows, even favoured the continental style of jumping, leaning back so far in

Oh The Styles They Are
A-Changing!
Left: In 1902 the fashion was 'continental', namely to lean back so far that the jockey's head all but touched the quarters.

Above: Today, today's style, – and today's crowds. Torrington in 1989. (Stanley Hurwitz)

Right: Early fifties, and the style was upright and long legged, hunting fashion. (Peter Pritchard)

the saddle as the horse prepared to land after the jump that their heads touched their mount's quarters.

Even the professional steeplechase jockeys rode very long, hardly shortening their length of stirrup leather at all right through the 1950s, and into the early 1960s. In the late Sixties it was not at all an uncommon sight at a point-to-point to witness riders with their feet level with the bottom of their girths. But when the change in length of leather did generally catch on, it did so not so much out of fashion but from necessity. Races were being run much faster and over stiffer fences, and the old upright hunting seat quite simply proved inadequate.

The man most widely regarded as responsible for the change in riders' position and style was the great Fred Winter. Assuredly there were great steeplechase jockeys before him, such as the illustrious and fearless Bryan Marshall, but since the last war there have been none, they say, so stylish. Nor any so brilliantly tactical. Nor, thanks solely to the growth of televised sport, so widely admired. Winter became to many a household name, and to the young riders watching in front of their television sets he was a hero, a star to be emulated.

What was to be copied was not so much his length of leather, or the beautiful balance he maintained through a jump or while stoking his horse up in a hard fought finish (and there were none stronger), but rather his superb positioning. He rarely ever wasted a foot of ground, ever mindful that distance lost early on always had to be made up, and that when it came to racing the shortest distance between two points was to be found on the inside. While riding he was also the best of sportsmen, modest, kind and always the first to congratulate his conqueror. To those learning their skills, his example must still be one of the most shining.

Plenty of good and some great jockeys have followed Fred Winter, many of them worth carbon-copying. But then imitation however flatteringly sincere is a purely superficial exercise unless the invisible parts of good jockeyship are learned, such as level-headedness, an ability to judge pace, and a sense of tactical skill. Riders may crouch beautifully balanced with knees cocked above the horse's withers, but if they lose all sense of purpose once the flag drops and the race is on, for all the good it may do they may as well ride upright and lean backwards over the jumps.

Nor is there any excuse not to be fit for the job nowadays. Not that there was good reason before, but with the contemporary emphasis on fitness, and the ready availability of properly equipped gymnasia, there can now be no plausible justification for unreadiness. Even so, certain critics within the sport express astonishment at the beginning of each season at precisely how unready so many people are for the task ahead, particularly when it is remembered how many races it is possible for someone to ride during one afternoon. Often under Rules a professional jockey may ride in six races, but never will that same jockey be asked to ride a card of six three mile steeplechases. On the other hand anyone aspiring to be a leading point-to-point jockey must expect to do so.

Exactly how the rider gets fit is a personal choice, but anything which strengthens the legs and the wind must be recommended. Swimming is excellent for keeping the body supple, while cycling, running and energetic walking help build legs and lungs. Some athletes blessed with naturally good physiques consider a sensible diet is all they need to observe in order to keep themselves in shape, which is nonsense, because diet alone is no substitute for a proper fitness campaign. Nor is a programme developing just the torso and arms with weights enough, since such a regime neglects the legs, and strength in the lower limbs is probably even more important than in the chest and arms.

Certain sportsmen are born with an advantage over others when it comes to their natural physiques, and those gentlemen keen to ride point-to-point who are no taller than five foot nine and have a natural weight between ten stone eight pounds, and ten stone twelve have been born lucky, for theirs is the ideal riding weight. There are taller jockeys, up to six foot five plus, but not many that much smaller, since the real lightweights usually turn professional. And as has been already indicated, with the exception of hunter chasing, and when claiming, men never have to carry less than twelve stone in a race. Therefore by the time a jockey weighing just under eleven stone *au naturel* has kitted himself up and sat on the scales, there should be little call for the carrying of much dead weight.

This is not the case for many of the girls riding, since the contemporary lady jockey is more likely to weigh nearer nine stone than eleven, and will consequently always have to carry lead. Many trainers, owners and riders feel this to be no disadvantage, considering weight is simply weight in whatever size or form. Others believe that too much lead in the weight-cloth is a hindrance, since it is inclined to inhibit the action of the

One of today's mixed races, both the ladies and the gentlemen. Alexandra Embiricos leads one of the sport's tallest jockeys Alan Hill in Div 1 of 1989's Coronation Cup, which Hill eventually won, on his mount Border Burg. (John Beasley)

horses' shoulders, and that 'live' weight is best. This led to a brief and unsuccessful experiment with a garment called a weighted vest, whereby the jockey rather than the horse was made to carry the extra weight. All this did was make the unfortunate jockey top heavy, as if he was riding in an armoured chest plate. Understandably the experiment never got beyond the infancy stage.

There is still a very strong school of thought which while grudgingly allowing women the right to race each other, still feels that they have no right to race against men. Most of the people admitting to this belief are most probably of similar background and descent to those who imposed the first ban on mixed races, back in 1929, an embargo which lasted up until 1967, although incidentally Ireland, so often considered by the British to be such a backward country, never once even considered such a proscription.

Others uphold this point of view because they feel that ultimately girls are simply not as strong as men and therefore

have no part to play in mixed races. On that argument alone then the only men who should be allowed to race against each other are those who are absolutely matched in strength, lest some be unfairly superior to the others, which of course is nonsense. If generally speaking girls are not as strong as men, then it is the girls who are disadvantaged by their weakness, not the men. Somehow, the results of certain races do not underwrite this, nor do they indicate that a jockey's most required attribute is sheer brute strength: absolute fitness perhaps, but Samsonesque strength not necessarily.

The real opponents to women racing unisexually, however, do not even make a pretence at being rational. They become inordinately exercised on the subject and proclaim that women simply should not be allowed to ride in Men's Races and that is that, the 'that' being because they are women. In this camp some will quantify their generalisations, by adding that women should not be allowed to ride against men particularly 'on unsuitable horses'. What makes for a 'suitable' horse is not described, but it is to be imagined to be either a horse which runs out at the first, or likes to go and stay last.

Others, capable of answering any other point without undue

Opposition to women participating in the sport has always been more than faintly ludicrous, particularly when the good female riders' skills are so apparent. This is well illustrated here by the participants at the Mid-Kent in the mid-Fifties. The hatless rider on the left was one of the best, Mrs Sheilagh French, riding her famous black horse Belsen Baby. (Kentish Express)

bias, have no shame at all in letting their prejudices show whenever this subject is aired. To quote one anonymous and otherwise perfectly sanguine source:

'Lady riders are excellent horsemen (sic) — the eventing world shows this. Yet in a race they go to pieces. The only explanation I can offer is that they are so involved with their horse, they are oblivious to what is going on around them. Certainly under rules they have had every chance and yet are remarkably unsuccessful. Someone once told me that they were there for amusement value — their own and the spectators!'

Attitudes such as this have led many to agree that the real reason some men dislike women racing against them is that they do not enjoy the experience of losing to them. The whole argument is self-defeating anyway, because if as some men try to make out women are not good enough to race against them, then there is no real danger of them being beaten, at least not fair and square. And if they are good enough, then they should in these days of proclaimed equality be allowed to take their place at the start.

1953 at the North Warwickshire, and the finish of the Adj. Hunts' Ladies', fought out by two great riders who enjoyed many a famous duel, Ida Croxon and Pat Rushton. (Peter Pritchard)

But no one can really be expected to believe that certain men are opposed to racing against women because they lose their heads, and are a subsequent liability. At least not when the unbiased observer has seen the wayward performances of certain male jockeys in closely contested races.

As for the courage of the ladies, this is surely undoubted by those of a fair mind. Their critics will call it foolhardiness, but again this is usually a case of pots blackening the name of kettles. What the ladies inject into the sport is a different sort of mettle, as those who have witnessed the best of their Open races will testify. They also introduce that element so essential to the creation of good drama, namely conflict, and the continued promotion of mixed races has done the sport nothing but good, at least certainly from the spectators' point of view. Whatever they fear, the boys would do well to remember that it is the girls who always have the last word. Just like the charmingly disreputable 'Skittles' (née Catherine Walters), a member of the *demi-monde*, who as a spectator created a sensation after the National Hunt Steeplechase had been run near Market Harborough in 1860 over a particularly fearsome course by jumping what had proved that afternoon to be a practically unnegotiable brook side-saddle and in cold blood.

'There's little point in thinking about falls because we're all going to have them.'

Brave words, but fatalistic ones, because with a bit more forethought some of the damage which can be sustained taking a fall may be avoided. There is, it is claimed as with most things, a correct and an incorrect way of falling, and the fair sex once again come in for criticism inasmuch as some say that this is another aspect of race-riding in which they are to be found wanting. When asked why this should be so, one leading lady rider replied somewhat tartly that the reason for this was that perhaps girls do not get quite as much practice at falling off as boys do.

There is, however, no doubt that when women do take a dive they do so differently to their opposite numbers, and that because of their difference in their advance reactions to the impending fall, they are more inclined to suffer injury. For instance, when they are about to hit the deck girls are somewhat more inclined to try and protect themselves by sticking out their

Opposite, above: If you can remember how to fall, this is the way: shoulder into the ground first, curl and roll. That is, if you've the time to remember. (John Beasley)

Opposite, below: This is copy-book stuff, too, although Miss Gail Harwood would probably rather still be on board. The need for back protectors is obvious here, as is the hands-over-the-head. (John Beasley)

arms, which is in direct contradiction to the advice on how to fall correctly, whereby steeplechase riders are enjoined when falling to put a shoulder to the ground and then roll themselves up in a ball. This makes perfect sense on paper, but is probably more easily learned through hard experience than careful academic study. Few novices instinctively fall well. The clever tumbler is the rider who has learned from study in the field.

Obviously there are certain falls for which jockeys, however skilled, cannot cater, and caught unawares they will fall flat on their faces, or stick out their arms and dislocate their collar bones. Neither can they be expected to do anything about horses falling on them, or giving them a hefty kick as they lie prone on the ground. What they can do in the circumstances of every fall is roll up and lie absolutely still until long after they think the last horse has gone on its way. In fact certain pilots, even if they are unhurt, wisely make absolutely no move until they see people hurrying onto the course to make sure they are all right. This way they can be quite sure the entire field by then has passed safely on its way.

Today's jockey will also be wearing the most up to date body protection, namely a padded and flexible undergarment whose design has improved enormously over the last decade, and which offers far greater protection against a passing kick in the kidneys from half a ton of galloping horse than did the fibreglass backshields of yesteryear. He or she will also be wearing the regulation helmet, (BS 4472), which although responsible for saving hundreds if not thousands of brains and indeed lives, does not yet include a contrivance for the protection of the rider's teeth. Perhaps before long a type of helmet will be developed similar to those worn by professional cricketers, which will adequately protect the face as well as the skull.

There are of course certain ways to insure against falls, and the first and more obvious of these is to hand-pick the horses which are on offer to ride. Naturally the apprentice rider cannot afford to be that choosy, as he or she will be anxious to get as much experience as possible. But it is well to remember that the best experience is to be gained on the best horses. All riding so-called bad horses will teach the learner is to avoid riding so-called bad horses. The chance to ride maidens should also be given careful deliberation. It will obviously be advantageous if the jockey is offered the chance beforehand to school the proffered horse, whereby the animal's jumping skill or lack of it may soon be ascertained. Whatever happens, the novice should never accept the ride on another novice on mere assurances that the horse is a great jumper. If he was that good, then the ride would most assuredly have been offered to someone of greater experience.

Next, riders with an eye on safety should always walk the course. Even when they are familiar with the track they should arrive in plenty of time to examine the entire circuit again on foot. Markers may have been moved since the last time they rode there, fences might have been rebuilt and made stiffer, or conversely they might be found to be softer and lower in certain places. The running rails (where existent) might have been moved out or in, the ground may be badly poached in patches, or because this is the fourth race meeting held on the course it may have cut up all the way round the inside, whereby it might pay the rider for once to take a line a couple of horses' widths or so nearer the middle. Bad ground on tight bends can lead to nasty falls. And it is a recognised fact that some of the worst falls take place on the flat.

Joe Hartigan, a courageous and talented horseman, in his excellent pamphlet *Your First Point-To-Point Horse*, illustrates the folly of not walking the track by an account of what happened to him when he arrived with time enough only to declare and get changed before riding for the first time at The Beaufort Meeting.

> 'By peeping outside the weighing room, it looked to me to be a straightforward set up of small "island" fences, well marked with flags. I flew over the first of these two small, well-made fences, then took a right turn to meet the third, which — although it was a hedge — was equally well-made and inviting. I was surprised to see the three or four horses in front of me rapidly slowing to a steady canter to take this one. Presuming it was a habit of point-to-point jockeys in the Beaufort country to go to sleep in the middle of a race (!), I charged to the front, put in a mightly leap at the fence, and then to my horror found I was on top of another fence. All we had time to do was somersault over it! The fences were placed in a narrow grass lane to form an "in and out" — a fact I would have known had I walked the course.'

Furthermore, in all the rides Hartigan had in subsequent point-to-points, this incredibly was the only fall he suffered, which most graphically underlines this important point.

Of course a similar disaster could not befall the modern point-

to-point jockey since courses are no longer laid out in this fashion but follow the regular pattern of 'park' courses with the jumps set out at certain intervals. Even so, things may change from meeting to meeting. Some courses have even been known to move the position of the finishing post, much to the consternation of the more ill-prepared riders.

So for the rider anxious not so much to play safe but to minimise the taking of unnecessary risks, a close inspection of the fences and the course will lessen the chance of falling. Connections may remind their jockeys time and time again that certain fences have a nasty drop on them, or the landing falls away to the left or right, but there is nothing quite like a close look at the fence *in situ* for the rider to appreciate the nature of the obstacles which are going to have to be jumped. It always pays to walk. There is no advantage to be gained from not doing so.

Walking courses helps jockeys in all sorts of other ways besides the minimisation of risk taking. It acts as a distraction before the forthcoming ordeal, and helps jockeys up-date themselves, by reminding them of where the course drops, bends, and climbs. A pedestrian inspection will refresh the riders' memories as to which bends must not be taken too wide for fear of losing precious yards, and where the hills lie upon which ground must

To paraphrase Cole Porter, he was a game boy, he stayed on and finished second. Tom Fowler held on and thus passed the post in the Old Berks Members at Lockinge in 1989 after looking every inch the winner at the last . . . (Stanley Hurwitz)

never ever be made up, even if the jockeys' horses are pulling their arms out at that point. Other horses, tiring horses may come back to them on a long climb uphill, but the jockey with a double handful must always resist the temptation to kick on past them. On foot, riders will also find themselves reminded precisely how long or short a haul it may be from the home turn, and exactly how many strides there are from the last in which jockeys may get their horses balanced and galvanized into making a final effort which will end hopefully in their being first past the post.

To return finally to the question of falls, it is to be noted that with plenty of experience riders also learn another important technique, namely how to anticipate an imminent tumble. When falls first happen, they happen so fast riders are not quite sure of the sequence of events and so can take no real evasive action. Soon they learn to recognise when the horse has taken a wrong stride into a fence, stood off too far or not 'picked up', and while not exactly determining there and then to bale out, the pilot will be aware there is every chance of a crash landing, so that if and when the horse suddenly seems to have no head, the jockey knows his mount is going down and ejects. Time and time again photographs taken of experienced jockeys mid-fall show them apparently 'stepping off' their tumbling horses, standing up in their irons prior to dipping their shoulders to the ground and rolling themselves up into a ball. But while this is perhaps not a consciously applied technique, for the seasoned jockey it most certainly is an almost automatic response. The practised pilot will have known a mistake has been made, will have recognised the point of no return, and will have prepared his or her exit. In the case of falling, forewarned is very much forearmed.

Oddly enough in these safety conscious days, at the time of writing there is no firm ruling on when an injured point-to-point rider may resume riding. Under Rules, professional and amateur jockeys are required to keep an official medical record, and after racecourse injury have to obtain permission not just from their own doctor but also from the Jockey Club M.O. before being allowed back in the saddle, whereas it is entirely up to the injured point-to-point rider to decide whether or not he or she is fit enough to compete again. The only restriction placed on point-to-point jockeys is under Rule 55, which states that:

> 'Riders who have had a fall must report to the Doctor in the Weighing Room and must be passed fit before they can ride again the *same day*.'

The inadequacy of such a ruling is plain to see. One of the commonest injuries suffered steeplechasing, under both sets of rules, is concussion. Under National Hunt Rules, jockeys may not ride again once they have been concussed without official permission. Under the Jockey Club's Regulations for Point-to-Point Steeplechases riders who sustain concussion may be banned from riding any more that day, but they may present themselves at another racecourse at the earliest opportunity should *they themselves* consider that they are fit and *compos mentis*. There is no official need for any further medical examination.

But since, as various medical dictionaries state warningly, 'each concussion probably puts some millions of nerve cells permanently out of action, and repeated concussion causes serious deterioration', it is recommended that 'anyone who has just recovered (from concussion) still needs observation, because symptoms of more serious damage may be delayed.' Furthermore, it is advocated that 'a doctor should be consulted in all cases of concussion because there may be more serious brain damage. Bed rest is essential, and the patient should avoid sports and work requiring concentration and skill until he or she is completely recovered.' Yet every season riders are seen to have falls resulting in an admitted 'slight concussion', only to reappear the following weekend, confessing when pressed to feeling a bit 'groggy' now and then, but otherwise 'nothing serious'.

Obviously there is a patent need for a reform in the Regulations here, because riders, particularly the more 'macho' ones, those old enough to have left home, and sometimes even those who have not yet reached their majority but are governed by particularly determined and ambitious parents may well choose to ignore any small but significant warning signs and return to the saddle far too soon, at serious risk to themselves, as well as to their fellow competitors.

Also, a revision of Rule 55 or more importantly an amplification of the rules concerning all injuries would relieve the riders of an unwanted responsibility. A typical dilemma facing jockeys is for them to have sustained a heavy fall one Saturday, and midweek to be offered the ride on a particularly good horse. In answer to the connections' enquiries as to their state of health, most jockeys, rather than miss the chance of riding such a good horse, confirm that they are fine, although in reality they have been undergoing intensive physiotherapy since the accident. Come the eve of race day, they find the sprain is not completely cured, yet rather than forfeit the chance of a win, they kid themselves that by the time the flag drops, they will be one hundred per cent, particularly with the aid of some analgesics or maybe even a 'jumping powder'. But in their heart of hearts they know they are doing no one any favours, least of all the owner of the good horse should its chances of winning be reduced by the undeclared and unhealed injury. No one can altogether blame jockeys for succumbing to such temptations. But the chances of such temptations being put their way would be greatly minimised if before being allowed back up, they had first to be pronounced match fit by an officially appointed doctor.

It has long been held that there is no point in beating a dead horse. Unfortunately there are some riders competing who do not give credence to this truism, and when their horse's race is done, are to be seen, like the infamous Capt. Clarke's half-trained mounted policemen, 'bumping around' on their 'wretched animals, with whips stinging off them' for the part of the race, 'and no chance of finishing anywhere!' A certain amount of blame can be laid at the media's door, for many racing commentators love to praise what they choose to call a powerfully ridden finish when what their euphemism really means is that a beaten horse is getting quite unnecessarily and unmercifully flogged. Modern television audiences have become accustomed but thankfully not inured to seeing jockeys prior to their return to the unsaddling enclosure carefully examining their horses' flanks for any marks which will tell of excessive use of the whip, and as a consequence of the public's reactions to the treatment certain professional jockeys are seen to mete out on their mounts, officials have been compelled and not before time to take very positive steps to curtail such flagrant cruelty.

Unfortunately, as well as being influenced to the good as to what they see their professional brothers doing, many learner-jockeys may also pick up some less attractive habits. Much as the Sunday footballer now feels the need to expectorate after every unsuccessful scoring attempt, so do many amateur riders think the riding of a finish necessitates the beating of their horses. Afraid of being accused of being soft-hearted, or worse — of not trying — they will be seen coming home with both themselves and their mounts hopelessly unbalanced due entirely to their wilful determination to ride a professional (sic) finish.

Some commentators are under no illusions as to how to redress this practice, recommending that novice jockeys should not be allowed to carry whips at all. This is a very well-intended suggestion, but they do not qualify it by stating exactly when the apprentice should be entitled to carry one. Certainly the proper use of the riding whip is learned only through experience, but it is surely a self-defeating project to ban jockeys from carrying whips while learning their trade, and then allow them to carry whips when they still have not learned how to use them.

It is held that the whip may properly be used on a horse that is about to run out, or one that is jumping dangerously, the thinking being that one good smack will make him at once come to his senses. This is somewhat dubious advice, although undoubtedly born from good motives, since it requires the administrator of the punishment to know precisely why in the heat of a race his horse is jumping recklessly or not jumping at all. It is also a recommended policy to give old and 'clever' horses who appear to be idling one or two sharp backhanders in order to make them buck their ideas up, but once again who can be quite sure before administering the whip that the horse is not running its usual race because it is in pain? A horse may be 'jumping dangerously' not from bloody-mindedness but because his back or pelvis may be hurting or because he has started to bleed internally. In other words, it is practically impossible to lay down a strict set of rules as to when and how the whip should be applied, if indeed at all.*

In fact the only people who can adjudicate as to the proper and improper use of the stick are the stewards, who generally speaking as far as racing between the flags goes have sometimes shown a marked reluctance so to do. Once again, few have spoken as coherently on the subject as Vian Smith.

> 'Point-to-point stewards seem reluctant to punish random riding by public censure or inflicting fines. Their instinct is to conceal; to avoid the risk of exaggerated publicity which public censure invites. They are not alone in supposing that where there is no formal condemnation there can have been no crime.
>
> 'Public protest can compel them to act. A few spectators gathered at a fence achieve more than they realise when they boo a rider who whips a horse in mid-jump. Their resentment draws attention to the act and makes it an offence. If the protests are loud enough . . . stewards can be startled or provoked into a summary exercise of their powers.
>
> 'This is not because they are weak men, nervous of "mob" opinion. It is because they are wise men persuaded to public censure because they are aware that no sport survives by right, only by consent. For that reason, if no other, the guilty rider is a menace to his own sport.'

The subject of stewardship will be returned to in a later chapter. In the meantime suffice it to say that the increasing vigilance of some of the point-to-point authorities is going a long way in helping to eradicate and punish whip-abuse.

It is also in the nature of an object lesson when it is considered that Fred Winter, although never averse to giving his horse a reminder when he considered it might be necessary, rode his hardest finishes through his legs. He was renowned for squeezing them home, and while it may be argued that in his heyday he

---

* Both Stan Mellor and Fred Winter were agreed that 'if a horse won't go for three (smacks) he won't go for thirty-three.' Furthermore, Mellor was of the opinion that if Marcus Armytage had not put down his whip after giving Mr Frisk a single reminder on the run in he would surely have lost the 1990 Grand National.

Left: Age is not the only thing the Corinthian defies.

Below: Mrs Sheilagh French, now a veteran, jumping the last in the Maiden at Hackwood in 1989 before picking them all off to come home the winner. (John Beasley)

never was given the 'dogs' to ride, it must be remembered that 'dogs', however hard they are beaten, do not win races. Winter, like Peter Scudamore today, could win his races 'through his legs'. Students of riding technique should study the way 'Scu' can swing the lower half of his legs to kick his horse on without, it seems, ever losing his grip. They should also note that there are few sights worse on the racecourse than that of an ill-mannered and inefficient jockey beating up a horse, whether it be a hoper or a no-hoper.

Not all offences with the whip, it must be said, are ill intentioned. In the heat of the moment, when jockeys feel victory would be theirs if their horses could just give that vital bit more effort, whips are resorted to rather than skills. Jockeys riding horses belonging to others might also be riding for the grandstand, inasmuch they feel the more ignorant of connections may suppose their pilots are not trying their hardest unless they are seen to be using the stick. But it is a spectator sport as well as an owners' game, and the public, however horse-ignorant they may be deemed to be by some equestrian cliques, have been alerted to the fact that certain of the indignities inflicted on racehorses are both cruel and unnecessary, and are prepared to be quite militant in their show of disapproval.

When it is considered that there are still plenty of people in their early middle age who still ride point-to-point and at the time of writing one or two whom it might be more gallant to describe as veterans (see the illustration of Mrs S. French on the opposite page), it might be applicable to ask at what age riders should draw the line. Perhaps the only answer to this is when it becomes impractical, both physically and metaphysically. Some riders mend quicker than others, and sometimes quite regardless of age. If someone wishing to ride point-to-point is the sort whose bones fracture easily and mend late, then perhaps racing is not the name of their game, whereas the strong and big boned jockeys may ride well into the summer and often the autumn of their careers with nothing more than a set of false teeth to show for it when they finally hang up their boots.

But it is a dangerous sport, and one which can inflict serious and sometimes mortal injury. So no one should partake in it who is not aware that there can be dire consequences. It is this very reason which causes many leading amateur riders to give up racing at the moment they seem to be at their best, simply

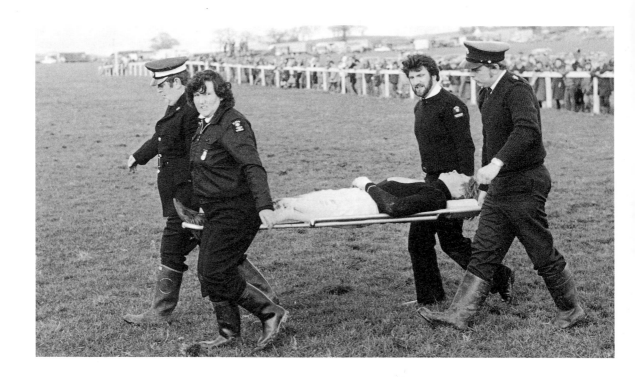

because by then they may have family responsibilities, or business ones which are now much greater than they were when they first started riding for 'fun'. Even so, it is a testimony to the sport and to the riders quite how many senior jockeys there are still riding, because since it is an amateur sport, they would surely not be doing so if were it not for the love of it.

The often unsung heroes, without whom there would be no sport. The voluntary workers of the St John's ambulance brigade in action at the Harkaway. (Stuart Newsham)

(A list of the leading post-war gentlemen and lady riders is to be found in Appendix 11.)

HORSES FOR COURSES
OR
THE PLACES FOR RACES

Earlier on, mention was made as to the importance of where owners choose to qualify their horses; this choice is not necessarily governed by convenience, since well intentioned owners if given the choice will decide to qualify with whichever hunt has the best 'Adjacents'. Adjacents are those other hunts whose country lies abutting the central one. Thus the Blackmore and Sparkford Vale's declared adjacent hunts are the South Dorset, Portman, Cattistock, South and West Wilts, Taunton Vale Foxhounds, Seavington, Mendip Farmers, West Somerset Vale, Devon and Somerset Staghounds, and Weston and Banwell Harriers. The prospective owner might live on the borderline of two of these hunts, or conversely right out of the 'country', yet choose to qualify and race his horse in this particular area because it contains the racecourses to which he considers his horses most suitable, and more importantly because it has the most adjacents.

This requires an explanation, since under Rule 72 (i) (c) each hunt is allowed an allocation of not more than ten adjoining hunts. However, without contravening the Jockey Club's Regulations, hunts with the healthiest list of qualifiers can find themselves 'adjacent' to other hunts who are not on their own regulation list of ten. Thus the Blackmore and Sparkford Vale, while not including the Axe Vale Harriers, the Cotley, the New Forest Hounds, the Minehead Harriers and West Somerset and the Quantock Staghounds on their roll of 'adjacents', are nonetheless deemed to be adjacent by those very hunts when it comes to the framing of their own point-to-points. These 'hidden' adjacents are very important when it comes to making entries, and so a very thorough perusal of the relevant Area Schedule is recommended, in order that owners and trainers may find out exactly where else their horses may be qualified to run. These schedules may be obtained before the beginning of each season from the Area Secretaries, a list of whom are to be found in Appendix 9.

Obviously it is essential for neophyte owners or owner-trainers to have a proper understanding of where their horses are eligible to run, and this may be gathered by a study not only of their particular Area Schedules, but also of the Schedules for their adjacent Areas. Should owners have horses stabled in East Anglia, it will be worth their while to study the Schedules for the Midlands Area (Lincs, Northants, and Notts) and possibly even the South East (Kent, Sussex and Surrey), while it will be to the advantage of owners with horses stabled in the West Midlands Area (Glos, Worcs, and Warcs) to send for Schedules from the South Midlands (Warcs, Oxon, Berks and Bucks), West Wales, South Wales and Monmouthshire, and possibly even from the Taunton Area (Somerset, Dorset and Wilts). With modern horseboxes, and on today's roads, ambitious livery yards think little of mounting raids on areas which in the Fifties and Sixties were still considered outlying, particularly when it is a question of horses for courses. For example, lady jockeys with horses not quite good enough to win the very hot Ladies' Opens in say the Taunton and South Midland Areas may find it worth their while making the journey to the South East where the competition is less intense. As may the West Country based owners of fast but sketchy jumpers find it advantageous to raid certain places in Wales and Cornwall where the tracks are sharp and the fences more forgiving than the ones in their immediate vicinity. There is a *caveat* worth noting, however, if a policy of raiding is to be adopted, namely that in certain areas of the country visitors although welcome, will not be granted any special favours just for travelling long distances, particularly if the visitor should find him or herself involved in a blanket finish.

Owners should also be aware when choosing the hunt with which to qualify their horses of how many races are to be run in their areas on the most suitable tracks. Some horses run better on one 'hand' or the other, so if an owner's horse is a long striding galloper who prefers to go right handed, and if the horse is to be qualified in the Taunton Area then it should be qualified with a hunt that has the most fixtures at Larkhill. In this instance it would be more sensible to hunt the said horse with the Royal Artillery, rather than the omnipotent Blackmore and Sparkford, since the RA host their meeting and are 'adjacent' for five (more at Larkhill). Whereas good jumpers with a shorter stride who do not object to running on a sharply angled left-handed track should be hunted with the Portman so that they may have the chance of racing four times at Badbury Rings.

Some first time owners may consider it an advantage to qualify their horse or horses with two hunts, in the belief that this alone will widen their range of intended targets. But this alas is a misapprehension, because all that will be gained by so doing is the chance to compete in two Members' Races, since under the Rules of Point-to-Point racing horses may only be deemed 'adjacent' once. The right to compete in more races can be increased, however, if the owner joins the British Field Sports Society, and the Point-to-Point Owners' Association, both of which bodies have their own races at certain meetings, and indeed the PPOA hosts an entire meeting with a racecard designed strictly for Members Only, while those who farm the land and are deemed to earn their living from so doing may enter their horses in Farmers' Races. There are quite a variety of 'category' races, even including one run at the famous Heythrop meeting for the sole and singular benefit of the *alumni* of Eton and Harrow.

It is ordained in the Rule Book that no meeting may consist of more than six races, except where special permission is granted to hold an additional Members' Race over natural country. Rule 72 also categorises which types of race must take place at a meeting, but the final choice when it comes to permissable options is made by each hunt's Point-to-Point Committee who then have to submit the design of the programme to the Jockey Club for approval. It is up to that committee for instance to decide whether or not to include the latest controversial invention, that of 2½ mile steeplechases for five, six, and seven year old maidens at starting. Should the committee decide against the inclusion, at the time of writing it cannot be persuaded to change its mind by the Jockey Club, since on introduction this race is an option.

Every meeting must, however, include 'one steeplechase confined to the hunt or hunts promoting the meeting', in other words a Members' Race, which in order of merit, is the easiest race to win on the card. This was not, however, the case in the first half of the century, when fields for Members' Races were considerably larger than they are today, and the competition for their winning much more intense. Those were the days when point-to-point jockeys were not so much specialised race riders as regular huntsmen, so the complexion of a Members' Race was more or less the same as any other race on the card, since far more bona fide members of the hunt rode in races than they do now. Today's fields for Members' Races are considerably smaller, sometimes absurdly so, with perhaps only one or two horses taking part, and more often than not with just one horse walking over.

The reason for this is to be found in the qualifications for Members' Races. Horses may only run if they have been hunted that season with the host hunt, but more importantly only if they are ridden by:

> The Master(s), Members, Subscribers, Farmers, or their respective spouses or children of the Hunt or Hunts concerned who hold rider's qualification certificates for the current season from those Hunts, (and) if so provided in the conditions of the race, Serving members of Her Majesty's forces.

Many of the jockeys riding point-to-point today do in fact hold qualification certificates from more than one hunt, some of the more determined holding up to perhaps half a dozen. But generally speaking pilots only hold 'tickets' earned by qualifying horses with a couple of hunts at most, and there are no longer quite so many people, be they Masters, Members, Subscribers or Farmers, who are either as willing or as able to ride in their Members' Races as there were in days gone by. It is, quite frankly, the exception rather than the rule to find as many as ten or twelve horses competing for the Hunt Cup, and so without doubt they can be categorised as the weakest races on the fixture list.

This does not mean that they are consequently the most uneventful or uncompetitive. For many the winning of their hunt's Members' Race is still a victory worth celebrating, and while some of the participating jockeys' styles might not be exactly copybook, their enthusiasm and courage is beyond reproach, with the result that the races they ride, although perhaps numerically small, often provide great excitement and interest, especially for the horses' local connections. Moreover, these races still allow the 'true' amateur a chance to race-ride, and even if the overweight and inexperienced pilot comes home a fence distant from the rest of the field, he or she will do so to a genuinely congratulatory round of applause from the equally sporting crowd.

Members' Races may have other inhibiting qualifications as well. They may for instance be restricted to horses which have never won a race under the rules of any recognised Turf Authority, or not for a certain period of time (usually two years), or for horses which have not won an Open Point-to-Point (including a Ladies' but excluding a Restricted Open), or if they are 'natural country' races, for horses which simply have never won a race, including any point-to-point. They may also have additional prizes or cups for the first non-thoroughbred horse or the first horse owned by a hunt farmer past the post, and very often they have both a Heavyweight division and a Lightweight one. All in all Members' Races can still be very colourful affairs, and undoubtedly they bear the closest resemblence to the original 'point-to-points', particularly those contested across 'natural country'.

As far as the rest of the races go, the placing of horses in them is more difficult than it is under full Rules simply because the choice is more limited. This may appear to be a contradiction in terms, until it is remembered that in National Hunt racing, because of the system of rating handicappers, it is a simpler task for the trainer to make sure of not running horses out of their class, and moderate handicappers can thus enjoy a fair degree of success through clever placing. The same thing applies to flat racing, but point-to-point does not allow the exercise of such politicking. Horses which have not ever run may do so in Maidens. They do not have to, since there is nothing to forbid a maiden from running in any other form of contest, but the principle is for horses which have not broken their ducks to do so in Maiden races. These contests are generally for maidens 'at starting', rather than 'at closing', which is to say that on the day of the race when the entry is made the nominated animal must not have won a race. This differs from National Hunt and flat racing rules, whereby novices may run in the same category of race throughout the season (viz. Novice Chases), without having to move up a class, although winners are rightly made to carry a penalty. In point-to-points, as soon as a horse wins its Maiden, it has to graduate to another class of race, a Restricted Adjacent, a

Restricted Open, an Adjacent or even an Open Race. Often a horse which wins its Maiden well will be aimed straight for an Open, particularly if the horse was first bought as an 'investment', for should it then go ahead and win its Open, its value will be greatly enhanced, and the connections should be able to sell on profitably. Should this happen in Ireland they would be able to sell the winning horse on with enormous profit, particularly to an English buyer, since in this country it seems to be the somewhat irrational opinion that the winner of any Irish point-to-point is worth six times more than the winner of any English point-to-point.

However, should the winning maiden be a more ordinary type of horse, the next step normally is for it to compete in either a Restricted Adjacent or a Restricted Open, which as the term implies, are races open only to certain horses: Restricted Adjacents being solely for those horses who have never won under Rules, and when point-to-pointing have never won better than a Maiden, while Restricted Opens are for those animals who have never won under Rules, and have never won an Open point-to-point, including Restricted or Ladies' Open races. Five year olds are set to carry 12 stone, and six year olds and over, 12½ stone. A horse then winning a Restricted Open at once loses its eligibility to continue contesting them, and again has to move up the ladder, the next rung of which leads it into the Adjacent Hunt class of race.

This is not considered altogether fair by a number of critics, who for some time have suggested that horses which have won a Restricted Open should be allowed to continue running in the same class of race for the rest of the season albeit under penalty, rather like winning Novices in National Hunt. There would seem to be little valid argument against this proposal, since, as it will be seen, the next two classes of point-to-point races, namely Adjacents and Opens, are very often framed with penalties designed to handicap but not exclude previous winners. Once a horse graduates to Adjacent and Open race class, the real system of penalisation starts, because in the two previous categories of races, horses which have won under Rules are not allowed to run, but they may do so in Adjacents, although they will usually be penalised for the privilege. Basically all horses entered in these races are set to carry 12 stone, excluding the usual allowances. Winners within the previous two years of each Adjacent race must carry 3lb extra, of each Open, (including

Ladies' but not Restricted Opens) 5lb extra, and of each Steeplechase or Hurdle race 7lb extra, the catch being that all these penalties are cumulative. Thus a horse which has won four Adjacent Hunt races in the last two seasons is set to carry an extra 12lb, and any horse which might have won just two hurdle races during the same period will be burdened with an extra 14lb. As with anything, it is always worth reading the small print on the race schedules most attentively, lest in ignorance novice owners should enter their horses only to find upon arrival at the course that their recently purchased ex-steeplechasers are set to carry not the 12½ stone they believed, but the impossible burden of 14 stone.

There is, however, when it comes to the placing of horses, no need for owners to adhere to an orthodox system of graduation. Many experienced owners enter their unraced horses first time out in Opens quite deliberately, in order to protect them from the mayhem of Maidens. In these cases their jockeys are instructed to follow horses which are well known good and safe jumpers in order that the novice horses may learn good and not bad habits. There is little wrong in this approach, always provided the horses are there to race and not merely to be schooled. Naturally and necessarily there will be an element of schooling when such a tactic is adopted, but then the same goes and sometimes much more blatantly so for horses running first time in Maidens. The point of the matter is that at all times the Rules of Racing are there to be observed, and the horse if capable should be given every chance of winning or of being placed should the chance arise.* This is obviously the drawback to running maidens in Opens, since it has often been known for the more precocious horses to break their duck by winning a moderate Open, and thus render themselves ineligible for Restricted Adjacents and Opens, and incurring penalties for Adjacents and certain other Opens.

Adjacent races, which were previously fairly straightforward affairs, changed considerably in complexion with the advent of sponsorship. They had normally been similar to Open races, inasmuch as they were 12st 7lb contests without penalties, the incoming sponsors, determined it seemed to prevent or at the

---

* In 1990 *The Sporting Life* started a campaign to draw the attention of the Stewards to horses which won their races immediately subsequent to being pulled up first time out.

very least to penalise winning Open class horses running in their races, moved the goal posts, and owners of winning horses found themselves with ineligible or heavily penalised horses. This was fair enough, if the desire of the sponsors was that new blood should be given a chance to win these races, but there is a built-in backfire inasmuch as most of these newly sponsored races, particularly races such as the grandly titled (and now defunct) South East Novice Championship, culminate with their finals being run as hunter chases on racecourses proper. Frankly the climax to some of this series often proves to be the very opposite, a farcical anticlimax contested by inexperienced and often moderate horses having their first sight of some stiffer and bigger obstacles in races run at a snail's pace, to the despair of regular racegoers and hunter chase fans alike.

Open races are marginally less complicated, since they are generally held to be as they are described, open to all. Nevertheless, on closer inspection of the schedules this is found not always to be the case, since some early season Open races, in order to avoid a gargantuan amount of entries, are limited to horses which have won or been placed in steeplechases or hurdle races under Rules, or in Open or Adjacent point-to-points. Besides allowances granted to mares and five year olds, Men's and Mixed Open Races are either straightforward 12st 7lb races for all concerned, or 12 stone with 7lb penalties for winners under Rules, or of any Open race point-to-point since a certain date. Ladies' Open races are framed likewise, the difference being the minimum weight without allowances being 11 stone, and the maximum or those with penalty being 11st 7lb.

Various Open Races are also now sponsored, Land Rover being the benefactors behind the first-class national championship for gentlemen, and the R.M.C. Group the ones behind the likewise excellent national championship for ladies. The Land Rover final takes place at Towcester Racecourse, and the Ladies' final, which used to be run at Chepstow, is now held at Warwick. Both these series are keenly contested and expertly mounted, as indeed is *The Times* Championship which is for Restricted Opens, with a final run at Towcester, and the Audi Grand Prix de Chasse whose final takes place at Cheltenham at what is undoubtedly the best of all hunter chase fixtures in the season.* There are many other

---

* Since writing, sadly we learn Audi have withdrawn their sponsorship as from 1990. No successor has been found as we go to print.

sponsorship races, but these are normally purely Area affairs, and details of the sport's generous benefactors and the races which they support can be found in every Area Schedule, which will also inform the owner and rider as to the local competitions and championships not only for owners and riders, but also for their horses, including free nominations to top stallions for the most successful mares. The other two major and national awards which must be mentioned here are *The Daily Telegraph* Cup for the most successful gentleman rider, and *The Sporting Life* Cup for the champion lady.

For a good while, certain enthusiasts have campaigned for the introduction of a handicapping system for point-to-point races, rather than the present habit of awarding penalties, the argument being that for winning certain types of races horses all get awarded exactly the same weight of penalty regardless of what horses they beat, and how and where they did it. Under National Hunt Rules, a horse which beats good horses impressively on a Grade A track can expect to have its nominated weight increased considerably the next time the handicap is assessed. In the meantime it will be made to carry a penalty. If however it should just squeak home from a mediocre field on a Grade C racecourse, the horse's weight will not rise that appreciably, at least not if the handicapper has been doing his job.

This of course is not the case with horses racing between the flags, where a victory is simply regarded as a victory and under most circumstances is there to be penalised. Naturally the introduction of a handicapping system would revolutionise the sport, and would be considered to be yet another administrative burden, while it might further be argued that it is not a dire necessity and that point-to-point racing has managed well enough without it up till now. But notoriously there is no smoke without a fire, and many owners feel some such system is long overdue, particularly owners of the winners of moderate and weakly contested Open races held at minor tracks, who feel their horses should not be made to carry the same penalty for winning as the victors of 'hotter' races at more notable tracks.

In fact the introduction of some simple form of handicapping might not prove such a mighty undertaking as supposed, in view of the fact that there already exist very thoroughly and assiduously researched form ratings and assessments, published annually by Messrs Mackenzie and Selby, and weekly during the season by *The Sporting Life* and *RaceForm*. The application of a handicap system in Adjacents and Opens to horses with exposed form would certainly bring the contestants closer together, and perhaps help limit the number of races which all too often turn into rather predictable and extremely unedifying processions. It would also help prevent the top class horses from scaring off the competition, if it was felt they were being 'brought back to their field'. And since suggestions for some sort of handicapping system have been aired now for decades, perhaps they are worth the attendance of more than half an ear.

Finally, mention must be made of the entry system, which for the novice-owner can be yet another black hole. Do-It-Yourself owners need to make all their entries personally, and even those with their horses in the care of livery yards should know the routine, since they may well find themselves called upon to declare their horse should their trainer be away racing at another course. The beauty of entering and declaring point-to-point as opposed to National Hunt is that owners and trainers do not have to make up their minds as to whether or not to run their horses until forty-five minutes before the race itself. This means that if there is some doubt about a horse's participation, it being dependent say in the case of a young horse on the possible size of the field, or in the case of an older horse, on the strength of certain opposition, the decision can be delayed until as much information as is available has been gathered about the competition. Experienced owners will have learned on the grapevine or even by direct enquiry where certain horses are running, as all good horses are almost always entered when possible at more than one meeting on the same day, and usually in more than one race at each meeting. This is particularly good politics at the beginning of the season when inclement weather can lead to last minute cancellations. Then by studying the entry boards which most racecourses mark up as horses are declared, the possible size of the field can be ascertained, and by politely requesting a look at the official card of declarations the exact identity of the runners so far nominated can be learned. Thus if owners are not very keen to take on the local hotshots yet again for fear of their horses becoming dejected they may decide at the eleventh hour either to switch to another race, or simply not to run at all and leave the horses in the trailers or horseboxes.

There are few disadvantages to this form of Russian roulette, except to note that the novice-owner will not be the only person playing this game, and thus care should be taken if the horse is intended to be a more or less certain runner not to leave declaring it too late, lest the owner is trampled underfoot in the last minute rush and fails to declare in time. If played right, however, there is great excitement and pleasure to be had from seeing whether or not the gamble has paid off, and the right race has been chosen for the horse at the right place and at the right time.

The other type of race open to the owner or trainer without a permit is of course the hunter chase. Previously in order to run a horse in these races a permit did indeed need to be granted by the Jockey Club, but that has since been waived and now registered owners have the right to enter their horses for these races, which are held on public racecourses, and run under National Hunt Rules and over regulation fences. The season starts in February, coincidental with the start of the point-to-point calendar. It ends as late as June, with the running of the famous and always well contested *Horse and Hound* Cup at Stratford-Upon-Avon.

Basically two types of horse compete in these races, the graduating point-to-pointer who has revealed its potential by one or hopefully more convincing Open race victories, and the experienced but older steeplechaser, who is taking a step down in class by going hunter chasing. The latter type of horse will usually prove the more consistent type of hunter chaser, since it will have had plenty of good experience over the bigger and stiffer obstacles, which will stand the horse in good stead, while the horse making the transition from point-to-points may well often founder or baulk at the larger fences, and leave its current form way behind it in the countryside.

The opposition will generally be tougher, too, and that, in conjunction with the increased height and stiffness of the fences, can often confuse and deter horses which have shown consistently good form between the flags. It would seem almost unbelievable that animals generally standing well over sixteen hands high should take notice of a three inch height difference, which is all there is between point-to-point and regulation fences. But time after time this disparity proves to be the undoing of what had seemed previously to have been bold but safe jumpers. Every season point-to-point horses arrive on the hunter chase scene preceded much in advance by their reputations, only for them subsequently to prove disappointments, while their seniors, often the very opposite of the young pretenders inasmuch as they have shown very little decent form when racing National Hunt, suddenly become rejuvenated by a spell of hunting and by racing in contests wherein they do not have to concede lumps of weight to horses with much younger legs. They then proceed to notch up a run of unbroken successes while the talking horses fall by the wayside.

But there is another sort of older horse which takes the step down in class and which strikes a note of despair in the true amateurs' hearts long before it has even run, and this is the horse from the yards of powerful professional trainers. This is a very contentious subject, and one which causes a certain degree of apoplexy both sides of the fence, for some small owner-trainers feel they have little or no chance against ex-Gold Cup class horses trained in Lambourn. They consider horses which have won as much under Rules as some which end up hunter chasing, sums often in excess of £70,000 steeplechasing, or over £100,000 under both sets of Rules, have no place alongside and at level weights with horses which in handicaps might be rated as much as several stones inferior, and that to prevent this there should be a line drawn with regard to prize money previously won, and that any horse which has exceeded the pre-set figure should not be eligible to go hunter chasing.* Furthermore they find the professional yards' defence that they only contest the more important chases to be no defence, since the 'more important' hunter chases are the ones that come with the pots of gold attached, such as the Foxhunters at the Cheltenham Festival which is worth well over ten thousand pounds.

The professional trainers conversely can see no good reason for not entering their horses in these races. From a pecuniary point of view they argue that the presence of a hunter chase on a racecard is detrimental to their professional financial health, and would be particularly so were they not even allowed to contest it. As it is they reason that most hunter chases are worth considerably less than the races which could and should be held in their place, and this is fair comment when novice hunter chases at some courses are deemed to be worth a mere six

---

* The 1990 season did in fact see the introduction of the rule forbidding any horse which had won a race to the penalty value of £6,000 or more from competing in point-to-points for two years after such a victory. For the 1991 season, the bottom line was redrawn, the figure now being £7,000.

hundred and fifty pounds. Furthermore the professionals argue, why should horses which have won good prizes but are no longer capable of so doing either through loss of form, slight infirmity, or simply increasing age be retired while they are still enjoying their racing. If they were still as good as they had been, they would still be racing full time, so the very fact that they have been asked to turn their attentions on hunter chasing suggests they are not the force they were and so therefore their rivals need not fear them accordingly.

Whatever the merits or demerits of the two arguments, the delightful thing is that the creatures in the middle, namely the horses, as always confound all logic. Because while all the flak is flying along come horses such as Certain Light, who ran but half a dozen times under Rules, winning once (a two mile novice hurdle), before being superbly trained by his owner Mrs Jean Campbell to carry all before him, in three seasons winning 6 hunter chases, and the incredible and rightfully famous Flying Ace, another privately trained wonder horse who never ran at all under Rules, yet won over 54 races to date including 23 hunter chases. The history of the sport happily is littered with David and Goliath instances, one of the most recent being Newnham's fairy tale victory in the 1988 Seagrams Fox Hunters at Aintree by a head over Shylock's Retreat and a field of twenty-two other runners which included Beamwam, Acarine, Eliogarty and Three Counties. It really would appear that the Jeremiahs in this instance were wrong, and that there is no such thing as a good competition without good competition.

What is undoubtable is that the overall standard of the average hunter chase has improved enormously of late. Previously, particularly in the Thirties, and after the war in the Forties and Fifties, they were by all accounts often semi-farcical contests, with badly schooled horses either cat-leaping the bigger fences, running out or simply ploughing through them. There were many brave and skilled jockeys, but there were also quite a few more than a little light on talent, and besides 'waving to auntie' at practically every fence, particularly the open ditches, they often lost their way between the hurdle and the steeplechase courses, got all too easily 'unseated' and not infrequently in their desperation to remount did so but on the wrong horse. Even nowadays there are one or two hunter chases per season which provide the punter with quite the wrong sort of entertainment, but these are happily few and far between,

thanks to the massive improvement both in the riding and the training of the participating horses, with the result that the hunter chase has to the broader of minds earned its rightful place on the racecard proper. And further to the argument concerning the participation of professionally trained horses in these races, it can be held that the presence of 'smart' horses in hunter chases has helped improve the overall quality of these contests, since decent horses scare off the sketchily trained and badly produced no-hopers, and insure that the well framed and prestigious hunter chase attracts the proper class of contestant.

It goes without saying that hunter chases are for amateurs only to ride, although surprisingly enough professional jockeys were in fact allowed to compete in them until 1928. The regulation weight used to be a level 12 stone, in order to allow the heavier owner-rider or regular point-to-point jockey the chance to ride over the bigger fences, but nowadays it is not unusual to find hunter chases with a starting weight of nearly half a stone less. For example, in the final of the Audi Champion

Waving, not drowning. Although a usual cause for mirth among the grandstand jockeys, it can be a lot better than pulling your horse's back teeth out when it decides to make a 'horlicks'. Miss H. Pavey staying aboard at Badbury Rings. (John Beasley)

Hunters' Steeplechase five year olds are set to carry only 11 stone, and six year olds and upwards 11st 8lb. Mares are allowed 5lb, and riders may also claim their allowances, which in full claiming cases may be as much as half a stone. Thus a five year old unpenalised mare ridden by a 7lb claiming jockey need only carry 10st 2lb, and while there are probably very few gentlemen amateurs riding able to do anything like that weight, several of the fairer sex could. Even so, gentlemen wishing to compete seriously in hunter chases need to maintain a lower body weight than if they were just riding point-to-point. The optimum weight stripped really should be no more than 10 stone, although most gentlemen riders would get through a season comfortably carrying half a stone more.

To date there has been an illustrious roll of honour as far as gentlemen hunter chase jockeys go, which since the last war has included such famous names as Major Guy Cunard, John Lawrence, (the present Lord Oaksey), Nick Gaselee, George Small, Ian Balding, Michael Bloom, Bill Shand Kydd, Bob McCreery, Sir William Pigott-Brown, Peter Greenall, John Greenall, Brod Munro-Wilson, Marcus Armytage, and before they turned professional, Brough Scott and Tommy Stack. The successful ladies are fewer, for although there has long been a line of fine female jockeys riding point-to-point, the most prominent and talented in the last forty-five years being Miss Jennifer Renfree (subsequently Mrs David Barons), Miss Pat Rushton (subsequently Mrs Pat Tollit, said by many to be the finest woman rider ever between the flags, and the first woman in Britain to ride 100 winners), Miss Monica Birtwhistle, later even more well known as Monica Dickinson, Miss Josephine Turner (sister of the seven times champion David Turner, four times Ladies' champion herself, and subsequently Mrs Bothway), the Misses Jenny Pidgeon and Alison Dare, and most lately Mrs Jenny Litson, few of them have made any great impact hunter chasing. The exception is of course Miss Doreen Calder, with her string of successes on her own Flying Ace, notching up nine victories in the 1988 season, and the most publicly notable has to be Miss Caroline Beasley upon whom immortality was conferred when the victories of her horse Eliogarty made her the first woman to ride a winner at the Cheltenham Festival and at Aintree over the Grand National obstacles. Recently Miss Katie Rimmell has followed in Caroline Beasley's footsteps, after being the runner-up on two previous

One lady who always shuts the pigs up. Mrs Jenny Litson showing her superb form on Mr Bosun at Larkhill. (John Beasley)

occasions, by finally winning the Foxhunters at Cheltenham, on her splendid horse Three Counties, expertly trained and produced by her grandmother Mrs Mercy Rimmell, besides winning the 1986 Chepstow Ladies' Final and the 1987 *Horse and Hound* Cup, but in 1989 Miss Rimmell had still to show her ability on any horse other than her one and only. Yet besides these, Miss Jenny Pidgeon who keeps a regular tally of three or four hunter chase victories a season, Miss Venetia Williams and the neophyte Miss Alexandra Embiricos, the ladies' total annual successes over regulation fences to date may still be counted on the fingers of one hand.

Having discovered in what races their horses may compete, next the novice owners and owner-trainers need to know the location and the peculiarities of all the appointed racecourses, whereby they will very soon discover the truth of the maxim about there being horses for courses, and vice-versa. There is no doubt at all that some horses are indeed 'course specialists', running up a string of successes at particular tracks while failing to produce their form at any other. This is sometimes due to nothing more than certain horses' partialities, but usually it is found that the reason why various animals run better at certain courses is because they are mutually suited. Some courses race 'short', and are suited to the quicker and short striding horses who are probably not genuine three milers, while other courses race notably long, and take every bit of 'getting'. The racing distance of these courses depends not only on their contours, or lack of them, but on their sub-soil. For example courses set on chalk obviously drain much more quickly than those set on clay, the former having the ability to absorb a week of winter rain and still return their going as good, while the latter after suffering a similar saturation might need to be described as bottomless. Therefore before deciding where it is best to send a horse, it is essential to consider all the course's physical aspects.

Since 1968 all point-to-point fences have had to be built of birch, but some courses have better built fences than others, with a higher percentage of properly fixed steeplechase type fences having a good thickness of birch, and a decent 'belly' of gorse. Others have no fixed fences but only portable ones, which generally are less stiff than fixed fences, and whose 'bellies' are sometimes made not of gorse but of fir, or perhaps even more birch. Portable fences do have one advantage however over fixed ones, and that is they can quickly and easily be repositioned to save the ground on both the take-off and the landing side. This is obviously of particular value to racecourses which host more than one meeting each season, for unlike National Hunt courses which have separate tracks for their hurdle and steeplechase races, point-to-point tracks run all their races over the same ground. Just one afternoon's racing can result in badly cut up ground if the going is soft and the fields for the six steeplechases are large. However good the maintenance, courses with a high percentage of fixed fences which host three or four meetings a year can become hazardous to say the least by the time the third or fourth meeting is held, particularly in the event of a dry spell.

The disadvantage of portable fences is that in their regular transportation from one course to another, due to the fact that hunts often share their fences, much of the fences' stuffing gets knocked out, and if the host hunt neglects to rebuild the shared fences then long before the end of the season many of them will be in a sorry state. By then there is little the course inspectors can do except order the fences to be rebuilt, and leave the hunts involved to decide whose responsibility it is to repair the damage.

Inspectors would of course be within their rights to rule that such fences were inadequate or dangerous and ban the meeting, but this is rarely the case, since it is hardly the fault of the hunt which has just inherited the fences, and it would be considered unfair to ban that meeting and make the host hunt suffer for the carelessness of its neighbour. However, the increased high standard of official vigilance, aided by the appointment of people such as ex-professional jockeys as course inspectors, has helped lead to a slightly healthier respect for the regulations, and has meant that the riders no longer need to take the law into their own hands quite as much as they did, as for example in 1965 when six of the leading Eastern Counties jockeys went on strike and refused to compete at the Newmarket and Thurlow meetings because they considered the Moulton fences far too dangerous.

However, there is still an unhappy tendency for certain hunts not to meet their responsibilities. These offenders, while happy to realise the considerable profit their point-to-point meetings afford them, have little other interest in the sport besides a mercenary one, and after their race meeting is over and done with for another year, pull up the tent pegs and lock the fences in a barn without as much as a thought for how they may improve on the meeting the following year. This is a reprehensible and short-sighted policy, and one which only helps to fan the flames of controversy, since many of those deeply involved in racing between the flags believe most sincerely that the future of the sport does not depend on the state of hunting's health. What is quite indisputable is that while some hunts are happy to encash the profits their point-to-point makes for them in order to support their often ailing organisations, they are considerably less than willing to put anything whatsoever back into the sport. Which is short-sighted to say the very least, for as everyone well knows, those that bite the hand that feeds them usually end up starving.

One of the main differences between point-to-point and National Hunt courses is the absence of the water jump. There are one or two point-to-point courses where horses are still required to jump water, but these are the exceptions. Regulation courses are also generally better railed, although many point-to-point tracks are now beginning to boast plastic running rails where their budgets allow. 'Banking' courses, long the favourite down in Cornwall, where instead of fences horses had to negotiate five foot grass banks, no longer exist anywhere in Britain,

Opposite, above: Badly made, and badly tended, this portable fence at Tatton Park shows both the need for Course Inspectors, and for Hunts to honour their responsibilities.
(Stuart Newsham)

Opposite, below: Better altogether. Well built and adequately 'bellied', with kicking rails and decent wings. (John Beasley)

although they are still favoured in some parts of Southern Ireland. It is mandatory, however, for all courses to have an open ditch, an obstacle which always appears daunting when viewed at ground level, but which if properly constructed poses no great problem to a good jumper well ridden.

Besides new running rails the better supported courses may also nowadays have white plastic safety wings on their fences rather than the more traditional versions fashioned from birch and sheep hurdles. All courses will have what is known as a safety factor for each race as well, which is the maximum number of runners considered safe in each category of race, and which is determined by the stewards of the meetings in consultation with their Clerk of Course and the Course Inspector. These numbers are constantly being revised, and are as a consequence now considerably more realistic as far as the survival and safety of more participants is concerned. This can be as large a number as 40 for a Members', Subscribers' and Farmers' Race over natural country, or as small as 14 for a Maiden, and is usually governed by the width of the jumps of the course in question. And while on the subject of the width of jumps, the first obstacle at each course is normally the widest, for obvious reasons.

What is most confusing about the courses is that despite the efforts of the authorities in 1983 to standardise the overall distances of courses into a uniform length of exactly three miles, there are still some enormous disparities. Eaton Hall in Cheshire for example, is a galloping course of 3¼ miles while the easy and under-fenced course at Fakenham in Norfolk is well short of the regulation distance. St Mary Hill, in Mid-Glamorgan, a charming and friendly racecourse, again is barely three miles, as can be judged from its average race time of 5min 57sec, the fastest in the country, as compared with the Cumbrian course at Whittington, which although flat is set on water meadows, rides a good 3¼ miles, and records average times of 7min 21sec. Time differentials can also be explained away by the going prevalent on various courses, and by the difficulty or easiness of the fences, but even so it is a known fact that some courses are as much as two furlongs above or below the recommended distance.

Many of the popular courses are roundly criticised for what appears to be poor maintenance of the ground. To some people it appears incomprehensible why those which hold the most engagements, and therefore technically should generate the

Opposite: Banking at Bray in Ireland. Banks used to be an integral part of British point-to-pointing too, particularly in Cornwall. But they have long since vanished with the regularisation of fences. (PC Photos)

most income should not pay better attention to the state of their going. Some explanation has already been offered for this, and while it is true to say that in some instances better management would improve the ground, in most cases it is simply a losing battle. No amount of harrowing and rolling between meetings, even if the weather permits, can possibly repair the damage inflicted on a course by up to and perhaps over one hundred sets of galloping hooves thundering across it in the space of four rain-sodden hours. The wonder is that given our climate so much good racing manages to take place on relatively acceptable going.

A full list of courses, and a cogent description of their plus and minus points, their character and their locations may be found in the back of Messrs Mackenzie and Selby's invaluable year book.

While wings have improved since the days of sheep-hurdles, it would be even better were they all to be made out of the same substance as the running rails in the background, i.e. plastic. (John Beasley)

THE ADMINISTRATION

'We thought because we had power we had wisdom.'

They say that within even the gentlest of people there lies a possible Nero, and certainly for most Englishmen it would appear all that is necessary to effect the transformation from bystander to *gauleiter* is the award of an official lapel badge and a bowler hat. At least this would seem to be the case with certain people who turn into petty dictators if given the authority to act as the officers governing a point-to-point meeting. There are of course many worthy, honourable, wise and competent gentlemen working in official capacities on point-to-point racecourses, but there are also regrettably still far too many members of the Old Boy network who do the sport no good by their clannish behaviour and by their lack of interest in the rule book. Nor does it help keep the faith when at major point-to-point meetings there are reported instances of only one of the designated complement of stewards managing to show up on race-day. Nor in these increasingly egalitarian times does it delight racegoers, concerned that the judges may have called the wrong horse in a close finish, to be told off like errant schoolchildren for querying the decision, instead of being attended to reasonably. Nor does it inspire confidence in a Stewards' Enquiry if one of the officers is seen to be physically incapable of conducting the investigation. Agreed, a policeman's lot is never a happy one, but official respect is not to be honestly and truly earned by the perpetuation of an officers and men syndrome. Respect for authority is only granted when that authority is seen to be on top of its subject, and when it shows itself to be both accessible and sympathetic.

In truth, all that a well ordered bureaucracy requires of its officials is diplomacy and a proper understanding of the regulations. Bureaucracies are after all invented to perform the public business, but unfortunately once they are established, it is said 'they develop an autonomous spiritual life and come to regard the public as its enemy.' Anyone who addresses themselves seriously to the sport of point-to-pointing would agree that this is very often the case when dealing with the authorities, who generally give the impression they are governing rather than guiding. Of course the administration of an amateur sport is fraught with difficulties. So much is dependent on voluntary help that personal idiosyncrasies sometimes have to be overlooked. Even so everyone who is properly involved with point-to-pointing agrees that the standard of stewardship is not always all that it should be. Various schemes have been suggested to help improve this aspect of the game, but they are generally all too idealistic and impractical, and it seems that the real answer to this ready ill is for the adoption of a more open minded and democratic attitude when it comes to appointing stewards.

Basically it is the job of the Hunt Point-to-Point Committee to invite those whom it wishes to act as the stewards at its annual race meeting. This is of course where the force of the local 'mafia' is most felt, as certain people, probably those with influence within the hunt itself, earmark the annual race meeting as 'their' day, and are accorded practically an automatic invitation to officiate. This is perfectly satisfactory if those selected are fit for and up to the job, but unfortunately this is not always the case. Passengers can be carried, but only if the majority of the nominees are well and truly experienced officials, otherwise the blind really do lead the blind. It would be laudable too, if perhaps one of the vacancies were to be filled by a new recruit, so that a register could be built up of 'trainee' stewards, and dangerous absurdities such as race meetings officiated by only one experienced steward with five others undergoing initiation could be avoided in future. The introduction of new blood is vital for the health of any sport, and none more so than racing, which often is in danger of becoming totally moribund due to its ultra-conservative nature. Certainly the hierarchy of point-to-pointing shows an unhappy inclination not to reinvite any newcomer to their ranks back again to act once more as a steward who shows the slightest maverick tendencies.

Naturally the improvement of stewardship is not as easy as it sounds, simply as there are not enough candidates with sufficient experience. This lack can of course be attributed to previous cliquishness, but whatever the reason there is a real shortage of eligible candidates. One excuse is that many of those who might make first class officials are too busy racing their

Perfect symmetry. An official blends with his background. (Martin Figura)

horses. This already poses great difficulties within the sport, since there are often very strong 'family' connections at certain tracks, either through officials owning competing horses or the participation of their kith and kin as riders. Some people hold that if there is a big family involvement in the sport, then this should debar any member of the tribe from acting as a judge or steward, but such a prohibition would unfortunately mean the disqualification of too many highly experienced people. Impartiality is therefore maintained by the simple expediency of a steward standing himself down for a race in which he may have a runner or a family connection. And if there is a worry that stewards whose children or spouses are jockeys may hold vendettas against riders whom they consider to have ridden one of their family off, then it is only to be hoped that the neutral balance will be restored by the disinterest of the other presiding stewards.

Of all the ministerial officials those most deserving of sympathy are undoubtedly the point-to-point judges. Without the benefits of modern technology, most notably any photo-finish equipment, and inhabiting in many instances somewhat eccentrically placed stands, these officers, frequently persons not exactly in their prime, are expected to demonstrate complete infallibility when deciding the results of races which are often very closely disputed by a lot more than just two horses. And more often than not their infallibility is questioned by spectators on the opposite side of the finishing line, to whom the result indeed appeared to be the very opposite. Unfortunately there is no doubt that in many cases judges have been wrong, but until a more precise method of adjudicating the finish of point-to-point races has been introduced their decisions have to be final. The hire of the type of photo-finish equipment used by official racecourses is way beyond the budget of any hunt, and at the time of writing there appears to be no alternative, although there would seem to be as yet unexplored possibilities regarding the use of the increasingly sophisticated Polaroid camera. A simple trip system set up on the most technically advanced Polaroid camera, the cost of which could be shared between hunts using the same course, might at least help settle a few of the more heated arguments.

The lack of a camera patrol also inhibits the passing of judgements on errant riders, although these enquiries naturally fall into the jurisdiction of the stewards. This is another grey area of stewardship, as has already been noted with regard to misuse of the whip. But abuses will continue as long as they go unpunished, and once again it is beyond any doubt that the authorities do not take a sufficiently tough line when it comes to penalising riding offences. Part of this is no doubt due to the perpetuation of the 'amateur' myth, inasmuch as it is not the done thing to lodge an objection, nor is it entirely proper to sustain one. That said, more riders do object nowadays, particularly those concerned with improving the overall standard of safety. Reckless riding is just as potentially lethal in an amateur race as it is in a professional one, and the dangerous rider is nobody's friend, particularly not his or her fellow jockeys'. Out in the country, or even nearer to home, without an official eye on them, some riders will take unnecessary risks, either through ignorance or just sheer foolhardiness, the more cynical of them perhaps taking them quite deliberately, safe in the knowledge that there is only an outside chance of a subsequent fine or suspension. And such cynicism will prevail for as long as it is allowed to do so.

The Clerk of the Course, unlike the Inspector, is also appointed by the Hunt Point-to-Point Committee, and 'is the sole person responsible to the Stewards for the general arrangements of the Meeting'. Among the Clerk's various responsibilities is one to ensure that 'all persons acting in an official capacity at the meeting have access to a current copy of Jockey Club *Regulations for Point-to-Point Steeple Chases*. The Jockey Club sends out a minimum of four sets of booklets for each meeting, and yet it is not unknown for many a 'person acting in an official capacity' at the race meetings not to have had sight of these up-dates, nor to be over-familiar with the book of regulations. What is even more common is for many MFH's to have absolutely no idea at all of the ordinances governing their annual money-spinner, and very little interest in doing anything constructive about lessening their ignorance.

And herein lies the major flaw in an otherwise well constructed hierarchy. As can be seen from the table in Appendix 1, the Stewards of the Jockey Club appoint a Point-to-Point Liaison Committee to carry out the work with regard to the sport on their behalf. And under this committee sits the Masters of Foxhounds Sub-Committee, run by a Chairman who is nominated by the MFHA but not elected by it. Theoretically the Chairman's appointment is for two years, but as history has shown there is very little which can be done to stop an incumbent from chairing the sub-committee for a very much

The course commentator's box at Larkhill. Not ideal, but better than the course at Woodford in Glos, where apparently the commentator was forced to watch from a tree. (Martin Figura)

longer period of time. The Chairman may also if he or she so desires elect him or herself onto any other point-to-point committee, and thus quite easily impose a form of dictatorship, with an in-built constitutional veto. This is only a grander way of saying that if the Chairman does not particularly like any ideas fed up to the sub-committee via the subordinate but more actively concerned committees, then those ideas will not see the light of day.

This sort of situation might be just about tolerable if the Chairman of the MFHA Point-to-Point Sub-Committee takes a keen and creative interest in the sport. But if the opposite should be the case then that presiding officer's position should be considered untenable. An out-moded and despotic chain of command will only hold back the sport's development, so it is necessary to fashion one more suitable for advancing it into the Nineties. For example, it is essential for the MFHA to make sure all its members are better informed about the sport and its developments, if the link between hunting and point-to-pointing is to be preserved. It is hard enough at present and will become increasingly difficult in the foreseeable future for positions to be maintained on anything except real worth. Autocracy has given best to meritocracy.

In fact those looking to the future suggest it is time that the MFHA revolutionised their thinking and made sure that hunting as personified by the hunts acknowledged with a little more grace than some do the part point-to-pointing plays in their continued existence. A study of the accounts of any hunt which runs even a moderately successful race meeting will reveal the size of the contribution. In Appendix 2 can be found the expenditure and income from an typical Bank Holiday point-to-point meeting, which shows a profit of over £10,000 at the end of race day. This is the sort of money made from a meeting attended by perhaps five to five and a half thousand people. Suffice it to note that on high days and holidays the more fashionable meetings are quite capable of attracting crowds well in excess of 20,000, which from the organising hunt's point of view, cannot – as they say – be at all bad.

The other officials appointed by the Hunt Point-to-Point Committees are the Clerks of the Scales and the Starters. A description of their roles can be found in paragraphs 24 and 26 of the Jockey Club Regulations. The inspections of horses' passports is now under the aegis of veterinary officers appointed by the Jockey Club, who have already been criticised in some areas for their somewhat over-enthusiastic approach to the task. On the subject of passports it is perhaps worth reminding owners and trainers that at meetings where it is mandatory to lodge passports prior to an inspection to try and remember to collect them before returning home, as some hunts levy a fee, or perhaps more properly a fine, of £5 should they have to send any passports back. Owners are technically responsible for making sure their horses' passports are up to date, although those who put their horses in livery yards will find the proprietors may well relieve them of this duty.

Dope testing is the responsibility of the Jockey Club, but since there is only the one 'dope-wagon', it is not yet possible to have the automatic testing of every race winner as it is under National Hunt Rules. However, the Jockey Club vet whose appointed job it is to arrange these 'swoops' hopes to deter any horse doping by not disclosing in advance which racecourses the wagon is booked to visit and when. It is also the responsibility of the

Here no evil, see no evil, speak no evil, if possible. Officials gather to discuss whether or not to have the blighter up. (Martin Figura)

Jockey Club to arbitrate on cases of dangerous riding which are referred to Portman Square, and to punish those who wilfully breach the rules. Offenders can earn themselves the sobriquet of 'Disqualified Persons' for a variety of offences, from ringing, bribing and doping, to the lesser known crimes of owning, training or riding a horse at an unrecognised meeting in Great Britain and Ireland (but not any more including ponies at meetings confined to pony racing), promised any reward (including expenses) to a rider riding in a race, or giving information concerning his own or other peoples' horses for monetary consideration. While 'disqualified' those persons cannot act as stewards or officials at any point-to-point meeting, enter, run, train or ride a horse, attend point-to-point meetings, or deal in any capacity with a racehorse.

As far as the administration of the sport goes, while it is true that matters have improved enormously of late, because things have got better does not mean they are perfect. Nonetheless, that said there is no doubt that a much more constructive attitude has been adopted regarding the management of point-to-point racing, and pressure is constantly being applied to hunts to make them more self-aware, and to compare their level of government with that of their neighbours. As it has been pointed out, some hunts are notoriously apathetic, and do the very bare minimum to get by from year to year, while others are actively energetic and creative. As with everything, so much depends on who is running the shoot, and if the Master or Joint Masters have the necessary enthusiasm and foresight, are keen to make improvements, and determined not to alienate their 'qualifiers', then both parties will benefit mutually. The Jockey Club seems anxious to make the hunts aware of all their responsibilities, and much as some would prefer to stand alone, unencumbered by a sport with which they do not altogether approve, or in which they have little real interest, few can afford to do so. And much as these self-same hunts may cavil at what they consider to be the constant interference from Portman Square in what were previously entirely their own affairs, the name of the game has been a long time changed, and as *Baily's Hunting Directory* had it as far back as 1962, 'it would be churlish to bemoan the change'. By and large point-to-pointing has served hunting admirably, and perhaps recognition of this fact is now more than a little overdue.

As for the Jockey Club, it is more than happy to continue its involvement with the sport and not delegate responsibility any more than it does now. As far as it is concerned, racing between the flags serves as an admirable inauguration to racing proper, since very often it is a family's first introduction to the sport. It is therefore in the Jockey Club's best interest to monitor the health of the game and to recommend and make improvements whenever possible and necessary. Because, as the Jockey Club is well aware, if point-to-pointing is to maintain its public appeal, it must be seen to be governing itself both properly and democratically.

RACE DAY

Terence Brady: Let's start by talking about winning. Because after all that's the object of the exercise.

Mike Felton: I don't know. Don't they say that anyone can win, unless there happens to be a second entry?

TB: True, but I'd have thought in the case of point-to-pointing that's only strictly true in Members' Races.

MF: Not always. At the Berkeley point-to-point the year David Turner won the last of his seven championships, there was an arranged 'walk-over'. It was 1984 if my memory serves me right. There were only going to be two horses in one particular but all important race, at least important as far as the championship went, and one of the horses in the race was David's. So he agreed to withdraw his and ride his rival's, thus satisfying both parties!

TB: But what about winning? How much does it matter to you?

MF: It matters inasmuch as I agree with that old bromide that says there's no point in coming second. You don't leave the weighing room and say in this race I think I'll only try and come second. If you've a chance of winning of course you go for it.

TB: And when you win you're a hero.

MF: When you win you're on a good horse. And when you lose you're a rotten jockey.

TB: You've been champion three times now, and runner-up. So you can't be that bad.

MF: I've been very lucky. I've had more or less first pick from two big yards, John Dufosee's and Henrietta Knight's.

TB: Of course. But however good the band, you've still got to be able to dance.

MF: It helps a lot when you have one and sometimes two really good strings of horses behind you, because then you don't have to ride the lunatics and the no-hopers.

TB: Everyone has to ride those in the beginning though, surely? If they're going to be seriously competitive. Or unless they're born lucky. Were you born lucky?

MF: I have been lucky, and I've had to work for it. I used to drive 90-odd miles every week to ride out and qualify horses for Henrietta Knight, and I rode one particular horse of hers for two years before she finally put me up. And my involvement with John Dufosee's yard only came about through the injury of his number one jockey.

TB: Is that the name of the game for most novice riders? Chance?

MF: Unless they're just going to be riding their own or their family horses, yes I suppose it is. You have to go around knocking on doors. Seeing who might need help exercising and schooling their horses. It doesn't mean you'll automatically get the ride, and it doesn't mean that if you do get it, it's yours for life, despite what some people may think. But if you keep your ear to the ground, there's usually someone starting out as an owner-trainer, or a big yard short of riders due to injury perhaps – people are always looking for work-riders.

TB: You came to the sport through eventing, so you'd been used to jumping decent sized obstacles, and local people had at least seen you in action.

MF: Event riders don't automatically make race-riders. In fact the very opposite's usually the case.

TB: I know. I once put an event rider up on an ex-eventer, and they both evented round the race course, and eventually both rapidly returned to eventing. But you made the transition. What was your first race?

MF: An Open, would you believe? At Nedge, in 1977. On a horse called Early Answer. On which oddly enough I'd been eventing.

TB: And what do you remember about it?

MF: My legs buckling as I dismounted. Talk about hard work. Yes, and the noise. I don't think anyone ever forgets the sheer volume of noise of their first steeplechase. One minute it's all very quiet. You're down at the start, way out in the country usually, hoping and praying you won't get 'carted'. The roll has been called, everyone is circling round, you're probably half a mile from the stand so all you hear is the jockeys' chit-chat, and the calls of 'No, sir! No, sir!' to the starter as you start to get into line, and then suddenly there's this explosion of activity. This cacophony. As perhaps over twenty horses thunder towards the first. In fact in my first race there were twenty-six runners.

TB: Sounds like a real baptism of fire. Were you frightened?

MF: You haven't the time. Not once you're running. You've been frightened, sure. You've probably spent the last forty-eight hours wondering how in hell you could get out of it, and as you walked from the tent to the paddock for that very first time, you just hoped no one could see how much you were shaking all over. But once you're up, it's that old thing – you just don't have the time. You have a fit racehorse under you, and as you canter down to the start, that concentrates the mind wonderfully. You have plenty of other things to think about.

TB: Particularly if it's a strange horse. Because even if you've schooled it, or ridden work on it, they're different animals once they're let loose on a racecourse.

MF: Correct. So you use that time as I've said to try and get the feel of the horse. See if he pulls. How he's handling the going. The butterflies start up again while you're waiting for your girth to be checked and your name to be called. But by then you're at the point of no return.

TB: The procedure at the start. Because of course you're not being sent on your way by professionals.

MF: The starter and his assistant like everyone else involved are amateurs. And if they're not that experienced at it, they can sometimes get bullied by the more experienced jockeys into letting the field off when you're ready (the experienced jocks) and when no one else is.

TB: Before the 'off'.

MF: When you get to the start, you give your horse a good look at the first fence, to remind the 'pros', and to wake up the novices. Then you have the starter's assistant check your girths, and circle your horse round until the roll call is completed. The starter will either call you out by name or by number, and you have to make sure you answer back 'Yessir!' loud and clear. Then you watch the starter and if you're a beginner, you don't take your eyes off the experienced chaps. You want to try and jump off in the first group. It's amazing how easy it is to get left behind at the start, and unless *everyone* falls in front of you, you just never get to make up the lost ground.

TB: Is there anything to be learned from the gossip down at the start?

MF: There's a lot to be learned from it amazingly enough. You'll often find out the shape of a race in advance, because somebody or other will say they're going to go on because

At the start and for once some extra help, as a steward lends a hand with checking the girths. (Stuart Newsham)

they're on a known front runner, and somebody else will say they're also going up front in order to give their youngster a clear view, so if you listen to the tactics as they're being discussed, you can often avoid getting entangled in a mad scrum to the first. It doesn't always work out of course, but more often than not you really can work out what sort of race it's going to be, and ride your horse accordingly. And as you get more experienced you can ask in the tent who's going to make the running.

TB: So homework's a big part of this. Even more so for the jockey than maybe the trainer, at least on pre-race day, and the day of the race itself.

MF: Yes indeed. Even though you're not going to know precisely who runs until forty-five minutes before the race, you can still sit down with the form books and work all the ratings out, and the recent form, and a few phone calls will give you a pretty good idea about who's taking which horse where and when. As the season progresses you'll know the way certain horses race, particularly since the majority of entries will be from your 'area'. And then once the field is known, as you're getting ready for the race itself, there'll be a lot more informative gossip about each horse's chance.

TB: It's not a sport wherein to leave things to the last moment. Except sometimes when it comes to declaring.

MF: The 'Declarations Game' is usually played most effectively later on in the season, when you can either scare off the opposition by declaring a good horse the moment you arrive at the course, or if you have a moderate horse which is entered in two or three races, waiting to see what runs in the first race, and therefore what your best chance might be. Otherwise everything needs to be done in plenty of time – as much as possible the night before. In fact you can do everything bar declare and ride the race itself the night before. You check all your tack and pack it.

TB: As in Appendix 4.

MF: Not forgetting your spares; particularly your spare saddle. This isn't something you think you'll need when you're starting out. But you do once a horse has dumped you and bolted off with all your tack and you have to saddle up another to ride in the next race, only to find you haven't got a saddle!

TB: So you're packed up, genned up – having made note of the bad as well as the good jumpers, and possibly any novice riders, and particularly any novice riders on novice horses.

MF: And most particularly any novice riders on novice horses who are bad jumpers.

TB: Then it's early to bed.

MF: And early to rise. Because I always like to ride out on race-day, as a loosener and as well as a reminder of the task in hand. Then over a light breakfast (optional!) I'll catch up on any news of which horses definitely run and which don't, run a final check on my tack, pocket my Jockey's Pass, my Rider's Certificate, and if it's a home horse, the horse's passport.

TB: Jockeys don't always get free passes, do they? You usually have to pay to get in and then claim the money back from the Secretary.

MF: It's a bit of a bore, but there's no other way round it, otherwise there'd be too many free passes circulating and the hunt would lose money. Okay – so I pack all my kit in the car, and set off for the course.

TB: What about the horse?

MF: I'm not taking a horse.

TB: Well I am, and you're riding it. So it's my job to get the horse to the races, which is something else you can't leave enough time for. He's been groomed, had his legs and tail bandaged for travelling, been plaited up, had his racing plates put on, which is something I do the day before simply because it's one less thing to worry about on race day, and coaxed into the horsebox. Inside the horsebox there's an old school trunk which has the tack which I have to bring. But you've still got the colours, because you rode the horse last. What happens if you forget the colours?

MF: You tell me off and I tell the Clerk of the Course which colours I shall be riding in. For which you or I don't get fined, unlike National Hunt, as long as I remember to inform the Clerk there's been a change.

TB: We're in the third race, scheduled for half past one, so I make sure to time our arrival so that the horse doesn't have to hang around in the horsebox too long, since the majority of point-to-point courses have no such things as stables, while leaving enough time for him to be walked after his journey, prepared without panic for the race, and for me to make the declaration. In an ideal world I'll even have left enough time to walk the course with you.

MF: I'll have arrived about an hour and a half beforehand and I'll definitely walk the course, even though I think I know it backwards. Today they've dolled off portions of certain fences since it's early in the season, but the ground is excellent and unpoached on both the take off and landing sides. I also notice which of the fences have been rebuilt since last year, and that because of the position of the running rail the turn into the straight is slightly sharper than before.

TB: If it was like the Heythrop Four Miler in which we all ran, you might also notice that the winning post has been moved another hundred yards or so up the hill.

MF: Right. Anyway on this day the finish is where it always is, and so are the flags. Which means I can work out my line more easily because I've ridden this course so often. On courses I don't know so well, or not at all, I'll rely on local information as to which way the finish rides – left or right, and what are the local bugbears. The Clerk of the Course is usually a great help here, as he'll tell me of any fence changes, or repositioning of rails, etc. Chums who've ridden on a course strange to me will let me know its idiosyncracies.

TB: Fine. So we've decided to run the horse. We haven't been scared off, and we're happy with the going.

MF: I'm not happy with the weather, because it's blowing a storm, and the rain is sweeping across the course. But then I've come prepared, since I know that about the only thing which stops this particular hunt from holding its meeting is an Act of God.

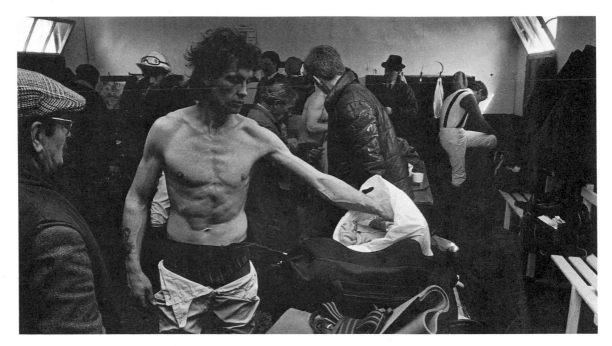

TB: You've presented your Rider's Certificate already to the Declarations Secretary, and I've filled in the declaration form, stating the time and name of the race, the horse's name, his number as on the racecard, your name as the rider, and signed it. I've pocketed the receipt, and then returned to the box to continue getting the horse ready. He's got his bridle on, and his brushing boots, now all he needs is what you're going to bring, namely a saddle, weight cloth, breast girth, ordinary girths, surcingle, and number cloth.

If he's wondering where the sauna is, he's going to be disappointed. Backstage, it's not exactly Cheltenham.
(Martin Figura)

MF: Time is always of the essence here. There never seems to be enough of it, even though as soon as I arrived at the course I reserved a place in the changing tent, left my kit in charge of the valet, and met up with a chum I'd asked last night to come and help me. A full afternoon's riding is mayhem. I mean if I was an owner-rider I'd be dashing back to the box now to supervise the saddling-up. Which is why it's so important to have a helper. On a busy race-day there's just too much to do by yourself.

TB: Anyway, people love helping out. They get a lot of fun out of being closely involved.

MF: You really do need all the help you can get. Particularly when you're starting out. Because most of the fine details you can only learn through experience. Such as how long it takes to get from changing tent to horsebox and back again. And the fact that you have to do it on the double. You really do have to run everywhere, because you can't afford to be late. If you're just about to ride a three mile steeplechase you want your mind to be concentrated only on that, and not on whether or not you've remembered everything.

TB: Even so, it is a punishable offence, isn't it – being late in the paddock with your horse.

MF: Yes, but most stewards are very understanding about this, particularly if you've been riding in the previous race. They know because of the logistics that everyone is stitched for time. Anyway, getting the horse in the parade ring in time is your problem today.

TB: It's my responsibility, but you're helping me saddle up. So I'm waiting for you. We've only got half an hour, so I take it you've weighed out.

MF: I have. It's important to know you can actually weigh out up to an hour before your race, which leaves you plenty of time if you've got yourself organised. It's also important for riders to remember they're responsible for the allotted weight. By that I mean it's up to you as the rider to make sure you weigh out correctly. For this race the only extra I have to declare is the breast girth, since the horse doesn't wear blinkers.

TB: And you don't have to put into the scale your skull cap, whip, bridle, rings, plates and anything worn on the horse's legs.

MF: And the compulsory body protector is calculated at 1lb less than the weight registered on the scale. But since the horse is carrying a penalty, I have my weight cloth, and am out at twelve stone seven, and on my way to the horsebox with the tack.

TB: And not forgetting the number cloth.

MF: Between us not forgetting anything, I hope.

TB: You used to have to saddle up in the parade ring itself, I believe. But now we're allowed to do it in or out of the horsebox. So on goes the breast girth, then the chamois leather, followed by a thin foam pad, the weight cloth, the number, and finally the saddle and surcingle which goes over it. And then we attach the breast girth to the saddle, making sure to leave plenty of room for the horse's movement.

MF: I always use an elasticated breast girth for that very reason, to allow for movement. And I like to girth up to a reasonable tightness, walk the horse round for five minutes and then do his girths right up before I get into the parade ring. Trying to tighten up fully in the paddock when the horse is getting excited isn't advisable. You're going to get a chance to check the girths again at the start anyway.

TB: You can over-girth a horse, can't you — particularly if you're using the elasticated type.

MF: Which is why I favour the ones made of serge. It's practically impossible to over-girth with them. But you're right, it is possible to over-girth. In fact Henrietta Knight was once told by an Irish trainer that you could make a horse break blood vessels by hoiking the girths up too tight.

TB: That makes sense. With too tight a girth, it'd be like racing in a corset. Now then. We've fifteen minutes before the 'off'.

MF: Okay. So I go back to the tent to await the call for jockeys, while the groom takes the horse to the paddock. What are my instructions going to be?

TB: We've discussed the race already in some detail, and now that we know the runners we have an even better mind's-eye picture. As we saddled up we talked even more, so all I need to do is go over what we've agreed, making a note of the condition of our main rivals.

MF: Generally speaking most trainers and owner-trainers will have gone over the race well beforehand. And equally generally speaking there are some pretty set categories of instruction. Such as to lie handy and go on three out, or make it all if you have to and start really to stretch them from four or five out — if he's a proven stayer with not a lot of 'toe' — don't make too much use of him too soon, and make sure you don't drop off the pace. It's not the most brilliant time to issue a brand new set of instructions, as you're being legged up and checking all is well. Anyway, if you've ridden the horse you know him, and if you haven't someone else will have, or you'll have seen it, or you'll have done your homework. The instructions in the paddock should, as you say, just be a recapitulation.

TB: You leave the paddock when you're told, not before, and not too long after. Although of course if you're on a difficult horse you can get permission to go down early.

MF: Today I go down fourth or fifth, I'm on a horse I know, and I know he feels well because as soon as he sees the exit onto the course proper he's taking hold and popping his cork. He was on his toes as soon as I got on him, so he's certainly 'at the races'. I have his girths checked and they come up one. I don't have to bother about his brushing boots because he's not wearing any –

TB: A word about brushing boots. And bandages for that matter.

MF: Yes, well some horses have to run in bandages, because they have dodgy legs. And if they do, the bandages must be put on properly, and fixed in place with tape, preferably. Bandages coming loose during a race can literally be lethal.

TB: But there are two schools of thought about boots.

MF: John 'Duff' never runs his horses in boots. He swears they're more trouble than they're worth. And of course when the going's heavy, you can put a few extra pounds on a horse during the race with all the mud they collect. They do prevent cuts certainly, in the hurly burly, and they add protection if the horse decides to hit anything, like a guard rail, etc. But if you're going to use them, make sure, just as with bandages, that they're put on properly, and taped in place. The other big word of warning, and why a lot of people don't favour them, is that if they're taped on with uneven pressure, in other words too tightly over the tendons, they can 'do', that is damage, a horse's leg.

TB: So all in all, more cons than pros.

MF: I think so. Anyway, I don't have to worry about them down

at the start, where I now hear that the favourite, who's a known front runner, is going to try and make it all. Which suits us as ours likes a lead. While I circle I watch the Starter and try to make my way to the inside to try and steal a berth up the inner. Quite a few of us are trying this stunt, but we judge this one nicely and as the flag drops I'm the only one off the inner. The horse has jumped off well and we're already second or third. The Starter's Assistant who's up by the first has dropped his flag as well so the race is on.

TB: If he hadn't dropped his flag?

MF: It would mean a false start and back we'd go again. Anyway, we're nearly at the first and I've a good sight of the fence. So I sit still and let the horse sort it out. The first can be a nightmare in lots of ways, particularly with huge fields, but today there are only ten runners and there should be room for everybody. Unfortunately the horse just in front stands off and our chap has decided to emulate him, and been half-lengthed –

TB: Meaning taking off at the same time as a horse who's half a length up on you.

Above: Not everyone wants to start in a line. Although, as was the case here, a good start's worth half a dozen lengths, as the first three, Paddy's Peril (no. 2), Fredwel (no. 9) and Nearly Handy (no. 20) are all in the front row. (John Beasley)

Opposite: At the halfway stage and the race is on in earnest, with the leaders all getting away from the fence well. (John Beasley)

The horse hits it hard and the jockey (Mr T. Woolridge) does well to stay on as long as he does, but the horse is going down regardless. (John Beasley)

MF: Which is exactly what we've just done – and he damn nearly caught me out. Which is what often happens at the first, horses copy each other, or in the melée get too close and have to fiddle it. Luckily our chap is very experienced and is a great 'lepper' so we clear it easily, and in fact land in the lead. I don't really want to be up front yet so I take a pull, so that by the time the race has settled into some sort of shape, by fence three, we're lying handy in fourth, and still on the rails.

TB: You look as though you're going easily as you pass the stands, and the front five are already opening up a gap of some six or seven lengths over the others.

MF: Right. So far it's going according to plan. I can see the favourite going on and jumping well, and there's only one horse here, the third horse, who wasn't in our reckoning. But judging from how he's jumping, it won't be long – in fact he's gone. He didn't pick up at all, and went straight through it, damn nearly bringing us down. But your little fellow's nimble, and he skipped round him.

TB: I thought we were gone. So did the course commentator. He called you as a faller.

MF: So I heard.

TB: You can hear the commentary?

MF: I always listen to as much of it as I can. Saves looking round to see how everyone else is going. Anyway, apart from a slight peck landing, we hardly missed a stride. The fellow who went through committed a cardinal sin. He tried to change direction into the jump, which is why we nearly went with him. You have to ride straight into the jump. Like we're all doing now. Straight in and straight out and now − on the flat − if I want to change position I may. In fact I'm going to because we lost the rails during that incident, and the horse in front is dropping back, and so I can safely, without causing any offence I trust, come back up inside and jump the next. Straight.

TB: You're third, about a length off the second horse but about six off the leader.

MF: I can see him, but he's jumping very left, away from how the track runs, and he's not getting away from his fences nearly as quickly as we are. But I can also hear someone closing.

TB: It's one of the unfancied horses and he's coming with a wet sail up the inside.

MF: Not if I can help it he isn't. I can hear him shouting at me to move over but we're still on the bridle and there's no way I'm coming off the rails for him.

TB: Three to go, and the favourite's come right back to you. It's any of the first four's race.

MF: Not the favourite, he's in trouble − and he's hit that one and disappeared. So now we're heading for the bend into the home straight, and it's a sharp right hander − so my horse and the horse outside me, we're both coming off the rail to flatten the bend − and I just hope this joker behind knows better than to try and come up the inside here. Because if he does −

TB: He is.

Above: What goes up must come down, with any luck still in the plate. Mr Simon Andrews shows circus-like skills at Tweseldown. (John Beasley)

Left: Coming off the last bend and ready to take the leader, if you're good enough . . . (John Beasley)

MF: I thought he would – and he's carried us halfway across the course. You can't do that. There's no way he could get round the turn like that. He's gone into me – and pushed me onto the horse on my outside. And now he's leaning. He can't help it probably, because his horse is unbalanced – and here comes the second last –

TB: And he's hit it.

MF: He hit it, but he's through it, and his horse is still leaning on me. And the jock's got his whip in the wrong hand and has just clouted me one. We've a touch of the meat in the sandwich here – so I'm going to save my breath and get on with it.

TB: You're getting away from the one that's boring you – but you're a good length off the leader coming to the last. You want a big one here.

MF: That's what you think. I'm going to take a pull – and steady him. To make quite sure of it – and we're over.

TB: And still half a length down.

MF: Better than going humpty. You don't win races flat on your back looking at the stars. Don't worry – we're going far the best.

TB: I can't see that, can I? And you're still only at the leader's girth and the winning post's getting awfully close! And now the third horse is coming again! Kick on for God's sake! Kick on, Michael! Kick on!

The three horses pass the post in a line. The commentator can't separate them. Nor is he allowed to for fear of influencing the Judge. And to guess from the ensuing silence, the Judge can't separate them either. Owners and trainers of both parties concerned rush to meet their charges to hear what the jocks have to say.

TB: Well?

MF: When I've got my breath back.

TB: You got it, didn't you? You must have done. You had your arm up as you crossed the line.

Left: Steadying at the last, rather than going 'gung-ho'. (John Beasley)

Below: Where everyone aims for, but doesn't always quite make: the winner's enclosure. But as most would agree, it's not the winning – it's hoping everyone comes back in one piece. (John Beasley)

MF: According to Mr Terence Selby that's something all point-to-point riders should practise for occasions such as this. We were certainly a good half a length up a couple of strides past the post.

TB: Here's the announcement. First — first number nine. Second number two — we've won. And third number sixteen.

MF: Who didn't do anybody any favours.

TB: He nearly carried you into the next county coming round the bend.

MF: Same thing happened last week at Badbury Rings. But in a much bigger field. We all came out wide on the final bend to flatten it, and someone thought he saw his chance for glory and tried to come up the inside. Nearly brought two of us down.

TB: What is the unwritten rule?

MF: If you're beaten, you concede the inside. Anything going better than you — move over. But on corners, particularly on sharp tracks, no. It's about as safe as overtaking on the inside on a motorway. Horses don't run on rails, and you have to make room on sharp bends. In the old days they'd have ridden that joker into the wings.

TB: Stewards' Enquiry.

MF: Ah. I should think so too. Mind you, if there hadn't been, and I'd been beaten, I'd have objected.

TB: Wouldn't have done you much good if you'd ended up on the floor.

MF: True. And it wouldn't have done me much good in the old days. But it's a little different today. I finished upright, and the Stewards are beginning to sit up and take some notice of what's going on out there.

TB: You'd better go and weigh in.

MF: Thank you for reminding me. Believe me, you can't be reminded often enough. Everyone forgets to weigh in at least once, and if you're going to do it, don't do it when you've won. I am now going to weigh in.

TB: Carrying all your tack and kit yourself. If you touch anything else, or anybody else, you can be disqualified, right?

MF: If it's not accidental, or unless you can show a pretty good reason, that's correct. Like none of the first four riders are allowed to dismount before reaching the unsaddling enclosure unless they're ill or injured. Or unless the horse has broken down.

TB: John Hislop recalls seeing someone being caught like that. The jockey of the second horse apparently fooled a winning novice jockey into dismounting as they were coming off the course, and then promptly lodged an objection, and got the race. Now horse and groom have to wait here till they call horses away, while I'll come with you because you've got to ride in the next race, and I promised to help.

MF: With all that rain, I should imagine I'll be a little heavier than when I weighed out – which I am. I'm a pound more, which doesn't matter, as I can be up to four pounds heavier before I get reported. Good – so now I have to change my colours, make sure what weight I'm carrying in the next.

TB: Twelve stone according to your card.

MF: Right. I must change my gloves which are soaking, and wipe my boots, and my goggles. And you can pour us both a cup of tea from that thermos.

TB: That looked pretty wet out there.

MF: It was. Particularly down the back straight, where the rain was coming straight at us. I don't think your chap likes the rain.

TB: At least he's going to be warm and dry in a minute, once the girls have seen to him. Whereas you lot – there's no such thing as running water let alone hot water.

MF: It is a little bleak, isn't it? Comes as a bit of a shock if you haven't been warned. I remember a friend of mine, after he'd ridden his first race, stripping down to a towel, getting a bar of soap from his grip, and saying 'Right, chaps. Where's the plunge bath?'

TB: What *do* you do to get warm and dry?

Rupert Nuttall weighing in, with his 'minder' ready to whip saddle and tack away to prepare for the next. (Martin Figura)

MF: Get into my car, put the heater on full, and drive home PDQ.

TB: While we've got a moment, tell me why you didn't go for a big one at the last.

MF: Why I didn't go gung-ho, you mean? And jump it like it wasn't there? Because that's actually how I was taught to go at the last. All or nothing. But I really don't subscribe to that any more. It really is asking to go humpty-dumpty, and you can often lose a race that's yours for the winning anyway.

TB: So you prefer to take a pull?

MF: I'd rather the horse saw the fence was there, met it on the right stride, and then got away from it quickly, hitting his stride right away, rather than ending up on the floor. It's got nothing to do with 'bottle', although the grandstand critics will say it's because you've lost your nerve. You have to think of the horse. It might be a youngster, and give him

'Gung-ho' at the last, and the consequences. Mr Ayres and Marathon Man wish each other cheerio. (John Beasley)

a crashing fall at the last – and believe you me, that's when you have a crasher, when you're going at full tilt on a tiring horse – you deck that horse and it'll be ages before he gets *his* nerve back, never mind yours. No, given the choice now if the horse has a good chance of winning, I prefer to take the last like any other fence and do our winning on the flat. And if it's a young horse and he's been careful, it's better to come second than end up on the floor.

TB: As far as riding finishes goes, the poor old point-to-point riders get an awful lot of stick about the sort of finishes they ride. But then it's not something you can really practise in the bath.

MF: You can learn a lot from watching the pros. You sit in front of the video and watch the top professionals and how they do it, and you can learn a hell of a lot. The amateurs' worst fault is we lose our balance. In the heat of the moment it's all too easy to start bumping up and down, and waving the reins at the horse, at the same time as you're trying to give him a couple of backhanders, and no it doesn't look pretty. You can practise though. You can practise sitting down and keeping your horse properly balanced when you're riding work.

TB: The de-briefing. If you'd been riding someone else's horse, how would you have dealt with the post mortem?

MF: Firstly, there's not a lot of time before weighing in, if you've been placed. And even if you haven't, you still don't want to hang around right at that moment. So it's the time for a few, but well chosen, words. Most owners like to think of their horses as swans, not ugly ducklings, so you don't get off roaring with laughter and tell them their horse would be better off pulling a milk cart. You try to be tactful, but realistic. If the animal jumped badly, you suggest a bit more schooling, perhaps. If it blew up, then you say it might have needed the race. If this is the third time it blew up, you might tell them it doesn't seem to get the trip, although really anything categorical you should leave to the trainer. Owners are there for a day out. They don't want to hear you bad mouthing their horses. But just as much if the horse has performed well, don't gild the lily. If it's going to win a Gold Cup it will do so without you looking into the

Opposite: Meeting the last perfectly. One of the most stylish lady jockeys, Miss Tabitha Cave, brings Camerata home to win the 1989 Tedworth Ladies' Open. (John Beasley)

future. It's all too easy to talk a load of rubbish about a horse's potential. And it's all too understandable too, if you want to keep the ride.

TB: You're more 'realistic' with the trainer, obviously.

MF: Yes. But usually after the races, or even the next day. Owners are the trainers' bread and butter.

TB: I'll drink to that. Because as an owner, nothing upsets me more than seeing the jockey going off talking glumly and deeply to the trainer, when he's just told me how potentially brilliant my maiden is. One last thing before you're called for the next race. As we were saying, if there hadn't been a Steward's Enquiry today, you would have objected.

MF: Certainly. If I hadn't won. And for once I'd have gone in there quite confidently.

TB: Which I gather you wouldn't have done not so very long ago. What's the form when making an objection?

MF: Following the lodging of your *written* objection to the Clerk of the Scales, or in other cases to the Clerk of the Course, within five minutes of the announcement 'weighed in', plus a £30 deposit, the rider or the owner, whoever has objected, will be called before the Stewards, where you will be expected to give a factual and concise explanation as to why you're objecting. You will then be sent outside while the other side of the case is heard, then the other party will be sent out to wait as well, while a verdict is reached. If it's a riding offence, and someone is found guilty, an on the spot fine will be imposed, or in less serious cases, a warning will be administered. If it's a serious case, it will be referred to the Jockey Club, but this is pretty rare, because not only does the potential offender have to travel to Portman Square, so too does the Senior Steward of the day! So naturally they like to try and solve it then and there.

TB: What else should the novice rider remember?

MF: Do your homework, do as much as you can the day before, including making a list of things to do on race day, because those first meetings are pretty jolly nerve wracking, and

Mrs Jenny Litson, able as always to treat those two impostors as the same, brings in the almost invincible Dawn Street. (John Beasley)

things get forgotten. And you look pretty foolish when you forget something publicly. And while we're talking about what you look like, you must dress properly. There's no excuse for looking untidy or shabby, with your colours not tucked in, and your boots still muddy from the previous meeting. Impressions count, and the first impression counts most. Yes — and if something's your fault, if something goes wrong in the race through your misjudgement, apologise. And not only to your owners, and trainers, but if you come up the inside, or crossed someone, also to your fellow jocks. You're much more likely to keep the ride if you're honest than if you try and pull the wool. And don't talk down to owners. If you're jocked off, it's practically impossible to get back on.

TB: The Championship. Suppose I wanted to set about winning the *Daily Telegraph* Championship. As a jockey, that is.

MF: Well obviously you need the horses. It helps if someone buys them for you, or rather for you to win on, like Ken Dunn did for Philip Scofield in 1988, because one good horse is not going to be quite enough.

TB: It's enough or certainly almost enough to win the *Sporting Life* Cup for the ladies. In 1989 Mandy Turner very nearly won the title with her ten wins on For A Lark. And in the previous year Jennie Litson won with sixteen victories, six of which were on Gathabawn.

MF: Which would have been seven if your horse hadn't carried him out at Nedge. To win the Men's Championship nowadays you need to ride at least twenty-five winners, and no one horse is going to do that for you in a season. Philip Scofield scored thirty-seven wins when beating me for the championship in 1988, and in the last twenty years, the least amount of victories needed was David Turner's seventeen in 1979. If you work out the average over the last twenty years it comes out at about twenty-six wins.

TB: To get back to this business of 'buying' the championship. Is that really on?

MF: Obviously you have to be good enough. Although you don't *have* to be the best rider to be the top one.

TB: It's interesting though, because in 1989 when Mandy Turner so nearly won it with her one horse band, the Ladies' champion Lucy Crow had the pick of a fair few horses. And I think mostly family horses.

MF: The family certainly gave her all the necessary support.

TB: What about yourself? Have you ever had that sort of back-up?

MF: Yes, to a degree. There are some family horses, Sutton Prince for instance, who's won sixteen of his last twenty-four points, and is owned by my mother, and I have a couple of my own, but mostly I ride other people's, and now that Henrietta (Knight) has turned her attentions to National Hunt, these come mostly from John Dufosee's yard.

TB: So given an ideal world, what is the recipe for winning a championship?

MF: You must ride right across as wide an area as possible. I try to qualify with as many hunts as I can, and since I ride mostly in the Central South and West Country, I qualify with six of the hunts which cover that area, in order to give me what we talked about earlier, as many 'Adjacents' as possible.

TB: They say the championship is to be won or lost in the West Country.

MF: Probably because the season goes on longest down here. It's happened before that the pretenders to the title have belted down West for the end of the season to try and pick up the necessary winners, to find they can only ride in two races. While if I've played my cards right I can ride in four. Of course you can have as many tickets as you like for all sorts of areas, but first and foremost you have to have the horses to ride there.

TB: And you've got to have the right horses, because let's face it, it gets pretty hard in the West Country for the last five or six weeks of the season.

MF: Correct. You need some pretty good firm ground specialists down here, and you need some good mud loving early season horses elsewhere. You must have at least three or four Open and Adjacent class horses, and even more importantly oddly enough, some good maidens.

TB: That seems like a contradiction in terms. How good's a maiden until it's not a maiden?

MF: By good maidens I mean horses who have had a 'prep' season, who've learned what the game's about, and should now go on and win their Maidens and their Restricted Adjacents. You need a good supply of these because they're your bankers. Then you must be prepared to travel. You're not going to win the championship by staying in your area. You have to enter everywhere, which means expense for your owners. Not like National Hunt of course, but enough to run up a bill.

Left: Gail Harwood and her father Guy enjoy the spoils of victory at Hackwood Park. Busy trainer that he is, Guy Harwood, himself once an accomplished point-to-point rider, still finds time to enjoy the sport he so obviously loves. (John Beasley)

TB: These multiple entries are to safeguard against cancellations I take it.

MF: Of course. It's all too easy to look at your local schedule and reckon on five good rides that weekend, only to wake up on Saturday morning and find the wretched meeting's off. And you've nowhere else to go. While if you'd been smart, and also entered somewhere up in the Eastern Area, and the West Midlands, and the South East –

TB: Poor old owners.

MF: You only grumble if you don't win.

TB: Fine. So you have your tickets, your horses, and your co-operative owners. So to achieve your thirty or so winners, how many rides are you going to have to secure?

MF: There are thirty-five racing days, so you're looking hopefully at about a hundred races.

TB: Bar a fall. There's your call for the next. Good luck.

MF: Thank you. Because that's the other thing you need to win a championship. Luck. And plenty of it.

Above: From little acorns. Easter Monday at Lockinge in 1984. Estimated attendance – 20,000+? And that was not the only meeting that day. (Stanley Hurwitz)

Today's meeting is a popular one, a holiday fixture, a fact reflected by the size of the crowd, which even though the afternoon is bitterly cold, with intermittent snow showers, must number well over seven thousand. Most of the crowd are sensibly dressed in layers of warm and waterproof clothing, showing them to be experienced point-to-pointers, because the rule of thumb as far as dress goes is before leaving the house always put on too much rather than too little, because you can always take off but you can't put on. And certain point-to-point courses are notorious for their 'chill factor'. On a cold day at Larkhill for example it is easy to believe that nothing lies between you and the Urals.

In fact generally speaking point-to-pointing is a cold sport. Until the middle of May is reached it is always possible the weather may catch you out, so therefore put on or at least pack away in the car plenty of extra clothing. 'Wellies' are *de rigeur*, as a look at the footwear this afternoon reveals, although one or two somewhat overdressed folk are to be seen trying to tiptoe over rather than through the mud in ordinary walking shoes. One or two of the girls in fact are sporting their regular black slip-ons, which are now caked in freezing cold mud, but they're trying to grin and bear it. Alas they will fight a losing battle, because no one wins with cold wet feet. As far as that goes, a great tip is always to carry your gummies in the back of the car, not in the boot. The novice's error is to do the latter, only to find on arrival in a car park six inches deep in mud that you have to get out of the car and slog all the way round to the back to get out your wet weather gear. To keep the feet warm, always change in the car.

From this it can be gathered that fashion is not of the utmost racing point-to-point, although the British, in keeping with tradition, have naturally evolved a fashion out of there being no fashion. At first sight this afternoon, upon looking at the assembled crowd, there would appear to be no common denominator in the matter of dress. Informality and practicality seem to be the keynotes, and most sensibly too when taking in the environment, but herein lies the key to correctness. Because going point-to-pointing the secret of modish success is not what you wear but rather what you do not wear. It is not done to dress up for these particular races, even or even more particularly if you have a runner. The stylist dresses drably, in Barbour Olive, Overlander Brown and Sloane Blue. Favoured materials are Loden, Old Tweed and anything Well Proofed, provided it is Heavily Distressed. Green, blue and standard black Wellies are all perfectly acceptable, as are those strange little modern galoshes finished in yellow and blue. They may be somewhat overbright, but they are perfectly correct.

Hats for both sexes are *de rigeur*, as can be gathered by another look-about this afternoon. The younger woman may be seen sporting anything from a Barbour hat, on finer days very often held in place by a chin-knotted scarf, to a beret, a snood, a cap, a knitted tea-cosy, or a broad ribboned Australian Overlander. The Antipodean Look has gained greatly in popularity, as witness the amount of both ladies and gentlemen wearing those slightly bizarre Ned Kelly type overcoats properly known as Drizabones. Gentlemen may also wear, and most commonly do, caps of various shapes and sizes, and the regulation trilby, known to the cognoscenti as a Brown Pig. These hats to be absolutely correct must never be pristine but must show signs of great distress, namely large areas of indeterminate staining and a profound shapelessness. They are not quite as fashionable on the point-to-point courses as they are on the racecourse proper, where the most correct example of the type is to be seen on the head of

Come rain, come shine, the bookmaking fraternity will still be there. (Martin Figura)

Mr Julian Wilson of the BBC. Point-to-pointers may quite properly wear tweed hats, particularly if the owners are members of the farming fraternity, but to be utterly safe sartorially in the headwear department, an old tweed cap would have to be the recommended choice.

Under the top layer of waterproofing various other layers must skilfully be constructed. Thermal underwear, or 'One's Dianas' as they are now more informally known, are of course a necessity. Latterly these were always referred to in somewhat derogatory terms, but now that they have come out of the closet thanks to their Royal Appointment, the county ladies take full advantage and spend many an idle moment on the course exchanging fortissimo jokes about their choice of unseen insulation. The more visible layers of clothing may consist of any variety of garment, as long as they are obviously distressed and of suitably muted hue. When point-to-pointing, one's things must never ever be at all bright or beautiful.

The venue of today's meeting is a natural beauty spot, although its natural beauty is not always easy to see thanks to the intermittent snow and rain squalls. Later in the season on a fine day spectators can enjoy magnificent views of the surrounding countryside, and this is yet another of the joys of the sport, for whereas many of the National Hunt courses were built in or adjacent to towns and cities, point-to-point courses mostly all stand on farm or estate land. Of course they are not all beauty spots. You rarely (if ever) meet anyone extolling the aesthetic virtues of Lemalla in Cornwall for instance, even those fortunate enough to lead in winners there. Viewing is appalling, there are only six fences (which have to be jumped twenty times), and it is adjudged most succinctly by the experts as 'not a venue for lovers of horse racing'. Tranwell in Northumberland, although a well-fenced course, scores nothing for charm, for all you can see of the action at Peper Harrow in Surrey you may as well stay at home, Mosshouses in the Border country is reputedly even more Siberian than Larkhill, while Marks Tey in Essex earns bad marks for poor officials, inaccurate judging, an almost total lack of Stewards' Enquiries as well as for its most unattractive setting.

These happily are the exceptions, readily outnumbered by the amount of courses whose settings, such as Bredwardine near Hay-on-Wye, are quite literally breathtaking. Nevertheless, for first-footers, even if they chance on a course set in an area of quite outstanding natural beauty for their point-to-pointing baptism, are bound to suffer some form of culture shock. Granted, there are some meetings which are held within the boundaries of proper racecourses and which can use their facilities, such as Carholme in Lincolnshire, which uses the stands, bars and kitchens of the old Lincoln racecourse, and the Silverton and South Devon meetings which are held at and can use the full NH facilities of the pretty Haldon racecourse. Tweseldown, since it was once a regulation NH racecourse, also remains one of the more civilised venues, although by now the utilities are certainly showing their age, but at least the buildings are of brick and not canvas, and the Ladies' loo is not inclined to blow away in the wind, as it does at many courses, most notably at Erw Lon in Carmarthenshire. Because that is how it is at most courses. Primitive.

Which is why newcomers' usually suffer an initial sense of shock, particularly if their racing days have previously been spent at such luxuriously appointed courses as Sandown Park, Cheltenham or Ascot. For point-to-point racecourses do not have their eye on providing for the spectator. The sport is run on a shoestring budget, and at the good courses whatever is in the kitty is spent on the upkeep of the course and the fences and not on putting underfloor heating in the Nissen huts. Very few courses have grandstands. Very few have even semi-grandstands. Most have no stands whatsoever, and the spectators must find out for themselves which and where the best vantage points are. At many courses there are no vantage points at all, and in order to catch any sight of the action whatsoever the crowd has to keep constantly on the move, clambering up and down muddy banks, running round the centre of the course, and peering and even clambering over hedges. Getting the best view at Tweseldown entails crossing the course to a vast mound in the middle, around which the entire crowd moves as one, backwards and forwards, and round and round in circles, as the horses appear and disappear from and into the plentiful and various thickets. At Nedge, high up in the Mendips, on a clear day you can just about see your hand in front of your face, thanks to the famous Mendip mist. On an exceptionally clear day, which are about as plentiful as direct answers from politicians, you can actually see the racing on the far side of the course. At Toller Down in Dorset not only is the start out of sight, but in the unlikely instance of you finding anywhere at all from where to catch sight of the racing, in order to witness the finish you need to be able to do the standing quarter mile in Olympic qualifying time. At Woodford in Gloucestershire, even the commentator – who apparently sits up a tree – cannot see the horses when they disappear from view at the fifth (which is also the fourteenth fence), at Kingston St Mary near Taunton again the start is out of sight, and so too is the all important action which takes place two from home as the horses career downhill and into temporary oblivion, while in order to view the contests at Hackwood Park in Hampshire, Messrs Mackenzie and Selby recommend the use of an hydraulic ramp.

At most courses too, it is recommended that the more sensitive racegoers should 'go before they come out', as what are usually referred to most decorously as toilet facilities are rarely all that they should be. For the Gents' loo at Lydstep, Dyfed, to merit the description 'primitive' makes the blood run cold, since how then to describe the sanitary arrangements at most other courses? Perhaps for 'primitive' in this instance one should read 'neolithic'. The woefully unhygenic public lavatories on the vast majority of point-to-point courses can only be attributed to parsimony on behalf of the organising hunts, since nowadays there are plenty of perfectly clean and acceptable portable comfort stations for rent. The trouble is hunts have to pay for their hire, and when a hunt can see a corner to cut, it cuts it. If the modest but highly satisfactory course at Llanvapley in Gwent, which hosts but one meeting a year, that of the Monmouthshire Hunt, can run to loos which actually flush, and can provide soap and running water, then what business has Larkhill, host to six meetings per annum, in having a Gentlemen's lavatory which does not even have a roof? And for how much longer will the ladies who attend the meetings of the Fernie and the Woodland Pytchley at the otherwise faultless Dingley course in Northants have to endure the shortcomings of its positively preadamite powder room? Even at the meeting which we are attending today, the Gentlemens' is a throneless and undersize tent, with trenches and troughs serving as urinals, while the Ladies' is in a precariously perched antiquated and reechy caravan. At many meetings the standard of facilities provided by the hunts smacks simply of cynicism and penny pinching.

There's not a lot to be said for the catering at most venues either. Not that people go to point-to-point meetings especially to eat, but when they are there they often find the necessity so to do. Those in the know pack a picnic, which is after all part of the tradition of going racing point-to-point. But some, usually the more casual or irregular racegoers, go empty handed and on a long and often cold afternoon they will need stoking up. It has long been a matter of international amazement what the British will accept in the way of catering, and nothing epitomises this more than the fare on offer at both our major and our minor sporting occasions. Go to any sporting event in other so-called civilised countries, and you are generally well able to eat without fear of being poisoned. In America it may only be fast food, but it is good fast food, and served good and fast. You can also get properly iced drinks if the weather is hot, and decent hot drinks if the weather is cold. On the continent it is likewise; in France you can get a twist of excellent pommes frites or a demi-baguette full of cheese or what you will. In Italy there are pizzas and pastas. In England there are soggy chips, greasy fried eggs in stale rolls, and headache inducing hot-dogs smothered in what appear to be boiled onions. If the weather is hot, so is the beer. If the weather is cold so is the paper-cupped tea. This time the fault lies at the door not of the organisers, but of the caterers. And of the

The modern picnic. One of the best ways to meet and entertain your friends. Because everyone goes home at the same time . . . (Martin Figura)

far too long-suffering British whose corporate attitude still seems to be that when it comes to food anything is better than nothing.

So better by far if and when possible to pack your own food. Look round you today and you will notice that picnics are not the prerogative of just the Hatchback set. The *al fresco* meal has long been part of the point-to-point tradition, ever since the times the country working familics were awarded a holiday to go and watch their landlords flash by across the fields and fences on their worthy steeds. There is an art to serving and making a good picnic, however, the rule of thumb being never serve anything that cannot be eaten one handed. For the true point-to-point picnic should be enjoyed straight from the boot or preferably the hatchback of the car. Some spectators may be observed setting up table and chairs, *à la* car park at Ascot. But this is not strictly correct and is considered to smack of the lay-by. Besides, maximum enjoyment point-to-pointing is to be had boot-hopping, so food which requires the attention of only one hand in order to be consumed is *de rigeur*, since the other hand will be required to be left free to hold the regulation glass.

Food should therefore consist of hot soup which may be taken from mugs, most preferably those won by collecting tokens from petrol stations, or those bearing more than slightly risqué slogans, served with hunks of fresh bread, and easily handled slices of home cooked pies, sausages kept hot in kitchen foil, jacket potatoes (ditto), chicken legs and wings, and a good selection of pre-sliced cheeses. Jacket potatoes kept hot in foil are popular not just because of their nutritional value but because on cold days they can double as hand warmers. Many a miserable pair of pointing mitts have been saved from frostbite by the clutching of a couple of pocketed hot tatties. Sandwiches are allowable, but only just and only if the bread has been decrusted and the final assembly does not weigh in above an inch in thickness. In fact anything in a roll, bap or bun is permitted, provided the confection is fresh and the filling flavorous. Old cheddar chunks and chutney butties are frankly quite uncommendable.

Needless to say, a well stocked drinks box is also *de rigeur*. Proper Picnickers prefer to carry and dispense their swill from those compartmentalised basketwork affairs which may be readily purchased from any shop ranged by the Sloanes, while the Fundamentalist prefers to make do with an off-licence box, still with its cardboard divisions *in situ*. A wide selection of drinks should be carried, both soft, medium and hard, because point-to-pointing is well known to occasion great thirst. There is little doubt, however, that the most popular drink is C^2H5OH, a volatile, inflammable liquor formed by the fermentation of sugars, and most favourably taken point-to-pointing by the fair sex in the form of sloe gin or vodka, and by the unfair sex in any form whatsoever provided it is not under 70% proof.

There are, however, some who should not indulge at race meetings, and the list must be headed by the officials in charge. Many of these gentlemen are no strangers to the nose paint, so much so as to occasion a request in the correspondence columns of *The Sporting Life* that it should be mandatory at all race meetings for judges and stewards alike to be dope tested both before and after racing. Such a measure would certainly prevent a recurrence of the type of incidents witnessed at today's meeting, namely when the judge gave the verdict in a tightly contested Members' Race to a riderless horse, and at an enquiry subsequent to the Adjacent a locally well known magistrate who happened to be the day's Senior Steward enquired of the jockey arraigned before him if he had any other offences to be taken into consideration before fining him £200 for dangerous driving.

Larkhill, Cup Final day. Hunts might not always be able to run to a television, but that doesn't mean supporters need to be out of touch.
(Martin Figura)

Riders too should not be encouraged to grease their throats, for fear of imbuing themselves with false confidence, and the subsequent belief that they can ride their horses through the eyes of needles, while owner-trainers should most certainly be counselled to abstain until their charges are home and hosed, particularly after an incident in the paddock today before the Maiden when a certain well-illuminated gentleman legged his jockey up and over the other side of his horse before blindly attempting to release the riderless animal out onto the racecourse with the bellowed instructions to pull up if they looked like winning. Above all, when celebrating a victory or drowning one's sorrows in defeat, always make sure someone remains alcohol-free in order to drive you all home. Dean Martin's advise can never be bettered. If you drink, don't drive. Don't even putt.

Besides eating, drinking and socialising, some people go point-to-pointing to watch the races, and more especially to back their fancies. There are some extremely serious students of form about, some of them almost fanatical in their devotion to the sport, as witness the earnest devotee to be seen today by the paddock and on the rails, with a large notebook in hand containing the details and records of every race run so far this season and the performance of every horse. Students such as this will know more about the horse sometimes than does the owner and sometimes even the trainer, and is not averse to having a tilt at the ring. And while it is a racing truism that no one ever put enough on a winning horse, some of these punters do very well, because it is also true that at certain times during the season the form of point-to-pointers is far more reliable than that of horses racing under full Rules. The reason for this is that the form is much more exposed. Between the flags the same horses are inclined to race each other with much greater frequency than National Hunt horses do, particularly if they are kept to race within their prescribed Area. Thus the good horses can quite easily set up long sequences of victories by scaring off the opposition. A run of four or five successive wins is not uncommon, and although the odds offered about such animals will invariably be odds-on rather than against, there will be occasions when evens, or 4/5, or even 5/4 will be on offer, and while these odds will be unattractive to the family punter, the serious layer will snap them up gratefully. One well known owner-backer is not averse to taking even shorter odds, being well remembered for a coup in Cornwall where he laid nine hundred to win back three hundred on one of his own.

He might not have been quite so ready with his money had the horse been a Maiden. Maiden Races are not good betting mediums point-to-point, just as Novice Chases are chancy under Rules. The serious punter is wary of the talking horse, and while Joe Public might well be tempted by the whisper about an unraced fancy from one of the major yards, and be quite prepared to take 2/1 or even less because the champion jockey has the ride, Mr Wiseacre will keep his money in his pocket until the Open races, which will provide him with more reliable form lines, and a more accurate 'market'. The bookmaker's boards are always worth watching, even for the most modest punters, because as the stables and owners known for liking a touch move in, the market will reflect their confidence, and on some occasions their lack of it. Some clever punters follow the gamblers rather than the horses, and by shadowing them round the ring discover who is backing what. These players are no longer surprised when they find a big stable or owner backing someone else's horse. They have long since realised this to be one of the most lucrative and potent form guides of them all, far more than anything they can learn in the paddock.

Paddock watching is for the so-called cognoscenti, for those who pride themselves in being able to pick the winner by adjudging its points. These people will tell you whether a horse be long in the gaskins, light behind the saddle, short in the stifle or too heavy up front. They will write off the little horse with the short stride and point out the right stamp of animal who somehow and mysteriously covers more ground with his hinds than he does with his fores. As far as the textbook goes, they will be one hundred per cent right, and as far as the consequent race-result goes usually one hundred per cent wrong. For the quality that wins races is not a visible one. What wins races is guts, talent, determination and heart, skilful training and brave riding. Which is why the paddock is of little interest to the serious punter. His eye is on the boards, and on where the real money is going. Just like a jobbing broker, he can and will play the market without any real knowledge of the commodity in question, which is, after all, why the pastime is called gambling.

Naturally the market is a considerably smaller one than it is 'in the parks'. The big backers know nothing of point-to-point form, neither do they have any real interest, because they know if they did decide to have a 'park-size' punt, the market would simply close up, unable to support bets of thousands rather than tens of pounds. Nonetheless, in the last decade, the size of the average bet in the point-to-point ring has increased quite astonishingly, and it is not uncommon now for a lot of money to be taken from the bookmakers' satchels, several of them the result of well organised and perfectly legitimate coups. These, and some other sizeable pre-season wagers based on the outcome of *The Daily Telegraph* trophy, are rumoured to have buried certain small bookmaking firms. There have been other organised coups attempted and sometimes successfully pulled off, but of a reprehensible nature, such as the running of 'ringers'. This practice of substituting look-a-like good horses for 'dogs' and then backing the supposed no-hopers in the past often went unnoticed, but thanks to the better all-round supervision and administration today, this ploy is rarely attempted. There was one famous case in 1980 which actually took place under Rules, but which indirectly involved the point-to-point world, when John Bowles was deemed to have swapped the useless In The Money with the six time winner Cobblers March to land a sensational coup. The winning horse was destroyed the next day, and Bowles was warned off for twenty years. However this did not deter him in the least, since by 1988 he was frequently to be seen point-to-pointing, and his name was linked with horses running in the name of one Lisa Smithson. He never tried to hide his presence at the courses and often refused to leave when confronted. The Jockey Club fined him heavily at the end of that season and Miss Smithson was warned off for twelve months.

As a rule though, it is not a sport which attracts the rogues. That there are some among the ever-increasing number of trainers and owners there is no doubt, but because there is no real money in it, point-to-pointing remains one of the 'cleaner' sports. And because the wagers normally laid at the average meeting fall into the category of 'family' bets, the bookmakers can sometimes afford to be a little more generous. They know that much of the money they take will be of the 'I-fancy-that-one-because-it's-got-nice-floppy-ears' variety, and that by and large when they're paying out it will be in fifties and not five hundreds. Yes there are bigger bets, much bigger ones, and while the amount wagered has increased by a staggering amount over the last decade, the point-to-point ring is still one of gambling's poorer relations.

Bookies are also normally opposed by a tote, and usually the hunt tote, although from 1989 onwards, the official Tote started appearing on courses in a rather smart mobile wagon. Formerly the only tote which appeared on point-to-point courses while most certainly a totalisator, was one traditionally run by a local organisation who prior to 1968 paid a rent to the organising hunt for the privilege of trading, an agreed 5 per cent of its total take. This to the hunts' way of thinking was not the most satisfactory of arrangements, particularly when attendances were down due to poor weather. Since 1968 a different method of levying revenue from the tote was arrived at, whereby the hunt tote paid a guaranteed sum, the amount of which was decided by averaging its take at the same meeting over the last four years. This was considered a much fairer arrangement since varying attendances and adverse weather conditions could no longer directly play any part. A glance at the mythical point-to-point balance sheet in Appendix 2 will reveal how much happier the new arrangement must make the organising hunt. Compare for instance the income derived from the tote levy (£750+) with the rather miserable revenue (£360) from a full complement of bookmakers.

There is little doubt that the bookies are not quite as popular as

Horses parade for the second at Oxford University's meeting at Kingston Blount. It may be an exclusively amateur sport, but there's not very much 'unprofessionalism' apparent. (Mike Roberts)

perhaps they would like to be, and certainly pre-1989 this was due to the somewhat disproportionately low rent they were charged for their site. Up until that year, for the best 'pitch' on the course, bookies were only charged £20 for the entry of their vehicle and for setting up their board, which was a faintly ludicrous amount when the public were being charged £8 to £10 just to gct in. 1989 saw a hefty increase up to £40 per bookmaking firm, but in return they were allowed free car passes and two free racecards per outfit. This did not go down well with owners, who have to fork out for a racecard at a meeting where they have a runner. The new £40 charge, although for once accepted by the bookmaking fraternity without a moan, was still not considered enough by many serious racegoers, particularly those who see the point-to-point course as no place for turf accountants.

In order to try and help justify their presence, certain bookmakers occasionally sponsor a race, for which the sport must appear duly thankful, but since the total value of prize money cannot exceed £250, their critics feel this is hardly going to burn a hole in the bookmakers' satchels. They would rather see the back of the bookies altogether, and all betting done on the tote. Naturally this would help swell the hunt finances, since the tote's rent is a reflection of its success. But such a notion is not all that commendable, since a tote strictly speaking is meant to be a non-profit making organisation, and hunt totes are often run by local organisations such as Rotary Clubs, who syphon off their own share of the proceedings. Better by far, therefore, to allow the bookies to stay and do business, especially now they have to pay more for it, until the day comes when the official Tote has enough Totemobiles to visit every course, and all the profits from their betting wagons are ploughed back into the sport itself.

The only real excuse offered for the continued preservation of the bookmaking fraternity which is seriously entertained is that without them racing would be a lot less colourful, a point which is difficult to oppose. There are for example no good stories concerning the Tote. But there are plenty about the opposition.

Like a delightful coup rumoured to have been pulled off at a somewhat obscure Irish point-to-point, on a three horse race, or rather a two horse race, since the third horse, a half-bred, was considered to have no chance as his price of 20/1 indicated. And which Mick backed to win £400 to £20. And which just before the off, when the money was pouring onto the two fancied runners, Mick backed him again, but this time on the drift, getting odds of 25/1 for the investment of the further £20 – just before the Starter dropped his flag.

Three fences out, the race was going as predicted, with the two well backed thoroughbreds two fences clear of the rank outsider, only for the favourite to run out at the penultimate fence, carrying the second favourite with him. The jockeys of both horses failed to redirect their mounts, leaving the half-bred to hack home and win as he liked. Consternation all round.

Particularly when Mick went to collect his winnings. The bookmaker was furious, and before paying Mick out demanded to know why he had backed such a patent no-hoper. Mick scratched one cheek and thought about it.

'Inside information,' he said finally.

'Inside information be blowed!' roared the bookie. 'The winnin' horse is my wife's!'

'Is that so?' replied Mick, poker-faced. 'Now there's a thing. My wife owns the other two.'

Try telling that about the Tote.

Now all that remains is getting home. And like all aspects of

The winner's enclosure at Chaddesley Corbett personifies the grass root connection and the friendly informality of the sport. (Stuart Newsham)

going point-to-pointing this in itself is an acquired skill. One certain rule of thumb however, is that when in a hurry, and having no runner in the last, always leave well before it. Few courses are easy to escape from, and if the weather is or has been highly inclement the chances are your car will have to be towed by tractor out of the muddy morass which earlier on had so optimistically been labelled Car Park. On days such as these, and if rushing home to dine with that other well known breed of stayer, namely your mother-in-law, start heading for home as soon as they have weighed in for the penultimate race. You will need to leave then, because not only will it take time for you to be towed out, but if you wait till the last the chances are that even if you do get extracted early, the impossibly narrow lanes that seem to lead to all point-to-point racecourses will be heavily blocked with other refugees.

If unhurried, the alternative is to rest awhile and wait till the madding throng has departed. But it should be noted that those mindful to leave last should be in four wheel drive vehicles, particularly if they have had a heavy picnic. People waiting for the crowds to disperse before leaving have been known on occasion to drift off to sleep, only to wake and find everyone gone, tractors and tractor drivers included, and themselves and family marooned fast in a sea of mud.

So how went the day? On paper it makes for depressing reading. Six wrong turnings on the way to a badly signposted racecourse, and a long queue to get in to a muddy car park from which it seemed there would be no escape, followed by a trek through a farmyard hock deep in silage effluent to a course where the facilities would have given even the Flintstone family a cultural shock. The initial sunshine gave way to an afternoon of sleet and snow, which made the limited viewing at this particular course even more limited, and as three total strangers contested a Members' Race which was even more unmemorable than usual, you did all quietly and in some cases not so quietly wonder why on earth you had bothered to leave the warmth of hearth and home.

And then a chum's horse won the Maiden in a canter on an animal you had helped him choose, and the party started. And then another chum's daughter won the Ladies' on a rank outsider, the stable where you keep your own horse had a double, and another chum rode the winner of the last, despite taking the final fence by the roots. By now you feel as if you personally had won all the races yourself, despite the fact that you had no direct involvement in any of them. But such is the camaraderie and the infectious enthusiasm, not only of your friends and their connections, but also of the other protagonists, that the afternoon turns into an equine *fête champêtre*. And on the journey home, you may all well reflect that en famille many a fine and dry afternoon has been spent going racing at one of the luxuriously appointed professional racecourses, but that never had you come away with the feeling you are all returning home with this evening, namely that wonderful and intoxicating sense of utter involvement.

THE FUTURE

As for the Future, your task is not to foresee it but to enable it.

(Saint-Éxupéry)

Having been written off so many times before, and with a mind to its history, the wonder is that the sport has survived at all. It was not all that long ago that 'Loriner' in his column *Off The Bit* for *Horse and Hound* (April 1963) was sounding the alarm bells. For despite good fields and first class racing, it seemed no one was coming to watch. At one mid-March meeting he attended he noted:

> 'there were so few cars and people present that I found it hard to believe that anyone had actually paid to come in at all: and indeed I later heard that the Hunt had not made one penny, a crippling disaster for Hunt finances. Usually, I understand, they reckoned on anything between £300 and £600 from their point-to-point.*

Spectators it seemed were scarce everywhere, even at the top meetings such as the Heythrop's. Loriner felt the real reasons for the decline in attendances lay not in the loss of some early fixtures due to the particularly hard weather but because of the parsimony of the bookmakers, the increase in entrance and racecard charges, the increased 'professionalism' in the attitude of the owners, who were blamed for only running their horses when conditions were right (!), the cliquishness of the hunting world, which continued to encourage townsfolk in the belief that the local point-to-point was a purely hunt affair, and above all else the woeful lack of publicity. People were complaining continually of missing local meetings simply because they did not know when they were being held, a criticism, like many of

* See Appendix 2 for an up to date comparison.

the others listed above, which is often still heard being voiced today.

Someone once described doing business without advertising like 'winking at a girl in the dark. You know what you are doing, but no one else does.' And for a long time this has been exactly the trouble with the sport of point-to-pointing, then and now. Certainly before, and not so very long ago either, everyone concerned with it knew what they were doing, but precious few else did. Attitudes such as this are born out of a fear of change, because change has always been considered anathematic to the diehards, who suppose it spells death to that which had gone before. And the adoption of such vulgar and commercial practises such as advertising race meetings would mean the very worst sort of change. For there was nothing the majority of organising hunts wished to preserve more dearly than the status quo. As far as they were concerned a body took an age to mature, but only moments to perish.

The start of the Tedworth Four Mile Open. Where better to be than Larkhill on a spring day with a winning chance under saddle? (Martin Figura)

Seeing the rude health in which the sport is today, with for the first time ever in 1990 over 4,000 horses in training and crowds of 25,000 plus reported at some Bank Holiday meetings, at first sight the reactionaries could be deemed as having won the day. But with hindsight this could well be interpreted as being the result more of luck than of judgement, particularly since television, the sport's greatest rival, surprisingly and somewhat providentially proved to be its greatest ally. Because television glutted the public with sport. It sated the home viewer to such an extent with its coverage of everything from football to show-jumping that a nation which for two decades had been happier to watch rather than do, suddenly cried enough and returned to the great outdoors.

In some cases people were inspired by what they had seen televised into going and trying it for themselves. But most had just become impatient of being armchair viewers, and were now anxious to get firsthand experience. And once bitten they were rarely reattracted to watching from their firesides. Anyone who has enjoyed watching sport speaks passionately of how very different it is when seen firsthand. For all its wonder and wizardry, the one thing television cannot ever bring into the home is atmosphere.

Point-to-pointing has also thrived on publicity, something the diehards would be loath to admit. There is no denying that the sport enjoys an ever increasing amount of media coverage, in the sporting press, naturally enough, but now also in the quality newspapers. *The Times* and *The Daily Telegraph* help to spread the word enormously, the former by its generous sponsorship of a series of Restricted Open Races, and the latter by the annual award of its challenge cup for the leading male rider. The championships are not the be and end all of point-to-pointing, but it is generally acknowledged that sport thrives on good competition, and whenever there is a near-run thing for either the mens' or the ladies' championships, more and more of the public consequently become more and more enthralled.

The majority of the organising hunts, alas, do not seem to have got the message, and their attitude to spreading the word is still by and large positively mesolithic. The norm is one boxed advertisement in the local newspaper and a billboard stuck in a field vaguely adjacent to the not very forthcoming attraction. The general reluctance of some hunts still to advertise what is usually their biggest money-spinner seems to stem from a presumption that those who are seriously interested in going racing will have got all the details of the forthcoming point-to-point season from one of the fixture lists printed in the sporting papers. These particular hunts never for a moment seem to imagine there might be even the slightest need to attract any new custom.

Proof of this can be gathered from a perusal of the balance sheets of any of the offending hunts' race meetings (see Appendix 2). The fact that most of these hunts appear to spend as much on prizes for the draw, as they do on advertising the forthcoming meeting, (namely approximately three per cent of their total expenditure, or about £200 out of a budget of £6,500) says it all. They appear simply to refuse to realise that the competition for their annual fixture is forever increasing, as each year finds more and more for outgoing families to go and see or do at the weekend. Last year's point-to-point attendance of 5,000 people will not be guaranteed again this year simply by the insertion of an inch and a half square advert in *Horse and Hound* and a boxed couple of inches in the *Southern Trumpeter*. In a world of rapidly increasing leisure time, attraction is the name of the game. The public eye must constantly be caught.

As a rider to this, there have to be plenty of attractions for the event to be attractive, which in turn means an enormous improvement of facilities. Twenty years ago Michael Williams was fulminating over the very same point:

> Hunts . . . have been taking too much for granted. It is not enough these days simply to put on a point-to-point fixture and wait hopefully for people to turn up for it. Much more needs to be done in the way of advertising and promotion. It is no good having something to sell if you don't know how to promote it. And it is no good at all putting on a poor programme with poor amenities. The public are much more demanding than they were . . . they are not much concerned with whether or not a horse has been 'genuinely hunted'. They want to see good horses and fair fields running over courses which look as if money has been spent on them. And they want to be made to feel welcome.

That was written at the end of the 1970 season, but it is doubtful whether or not at certain courses the author would notice that much change two decades later. Which is more than faintly bemusing when the increasing size of some hunts' profits are taken into account. At the present time the sport is enjoying another of its boom periods, and even some small hunts which might otherwise be struggling or forced into realising their greatest nightmare, namely that of amalgamation, are managing to stay afloat thanks to the money made from their point-to-point meetings. It should be noted that as a general rule, of listed contributions of say £20,000 pa besides income from hunting, a good twenty per cent of this sum comes from the hunt's annual race meeting, and from the subscriptions and caps paid by qualifiers,* while the more affluent hunts, particularly those fortunate enough to hold their meetings on a public holiday, can whistle all the way to the bank to the tune of five times that amount. Yet precious little of these profits are ploughed back into the sport itself. Much to their discredit, the offending hunts are simply prepared well enough to take, but quite unready to give, convincing themselves and their committees that what was good enough for this year will therefore still be good enough for next year. After all, they argue, you only call the vet out if the horse is lame, not if it's sound.

But this no longer holds in the world today. In the top professional training yards, the veterinarians are called in weekly to make sure the horses stay in good health. In order to ascertain this, blood counts are taken, and hearts are listened to. Good medicine now not only cures but also prevents. The same goes in the mechanical world. Preventative maintenance is now undertaken in order to forestall avoidable breakdowns. In fact foresight is the name of the game for those who believe that forewarned is forearmed, and the errant hunts should take note of this point.

They will no doubt argue the point has been duly taken but no action is yet necessary because of the ever increasing attendances, the ready availability of new sponsors, and the amount of new money being poured into the sport. Furthermore, as soon as the gaming laws are straightened out there will be Sunday point-to-point racing, as there is in Ireland, where the sport also has never been in better shape. And once there is Sunday racing the crowds will increase even more, as there will no longer be any more of those unfortunate and economically damaging clashes

---

* In certain hunts where as many as two dozen or more racehorses are qualified, allowing for £200 per animal plus caps, at least £7,500+ from this source alone will find its way into the hunt coffers.

on Saturdays between local meetings. On all known evidence, the prognosis can only be a healthy one.

For point-to-pointing perhaps, yes. But as far as hunting goes, alas not necessarily. Particularly if hunting refuses to heed the danger said to be coming from Europe. For the rumours are that European legislation could well bring about an end to hunting, since the aim of the European community is something somewhat euphemistically labelled as 'harmonisation', but which is generally taken by the cynics to mean conformity rather than concord.

One of the EEC's targets for 'harmonisation' in these ecologically minded times is predictably enough the environment. And since foxhunting on the continent is virtually non-existent, naturally it has few supporters. But make no mistake, among the citizens of countries who shoot songbirds for pleasure, it has plenty of enemies. Enoch Powell, a man who loves to ride to hounds, was one of the first to sound the alarm.

> Those who already voted to harmonise the standard of bathing beaches will vote to harmonise hunting as soon as look at you . . . Who shall decide whether it is forbidden by law in Britain to ride to hounds? . . . Alas, the plain citizen does not know what has changed while he was taking no notice. He has ceased to be the free citizen of a country governed by those responsible to him in his own free parliament.

How right he was to draw the attention of interested parties to what was happening, or more properly what could be about to happen, was shown in 1989 when proposals put forward by a Dutch Socialist MEP to restrict hunting in the Community were approved in the European Parliament by 177 votes to 38, a majority of 139. In the same year a German Socialist MEP demanded legal action against events involving cruelty to animals, singling out, it should be noted, not only hunting but also the Grand National. It does not take a very big leap of the imagination to see what else such proposals could embrace were they ever to become European legislation.

Fortunately even before these proposals had reached the report stage in the European Parliament, the British Fields Sports Society was at work, already alarmed by the threat of attack. The

BFSS made Europe 'a priority for its work' according to the Society's European consultant Maria Laptev, who personally argued that the threat against Field Sports could only be curtailed by energetic and coherent lobbying from the hunting fraternity. The call to arms was urgent, for much of the rural way of life which had resisted and survived fourteen years of Socialist government stood once again seriously endangered.

In order to resist this threat to its future, hunting is going to need all the friends it can get, and it has to be faced, outside its own particular world, in these green and ecologically minded times it does not have that many, however green and ecologically minded hunting tries to paint itself. By and large country people accept the role hunting plays in preserving the balance of the countryside, but there are plenty of others who find it hard to equate what they see as blood sports with conservation, so besides the BFSS, hunting would appear to be a little short of organised support.

Which is perhaps why the time has come for the more reactionary hunts to revise their attitudes towards point-to-pointing. They would only help themselves by acknowledging the value of the contribution not only of those among their subscribers who qualify racehorses, but also of the public who come and support the hunts' main annual money-spinners. Continued imperiousness can only be detrimental to hunting's health, and perhaps even fatally so, for after all, as it has already been indicated, it is not inconceivable that point-to-pointing could continue to exist without the support of hunting, but in these straightened and now threatened times it is getting harder and harder to imagine hunting being able to survive without point-to-pointing's financial input, and in terms of any forth-coming European debate, without the sport's wholehearted support. Few on either side would welcome such a time, but more than a few can foresee it.

While point-to-pointing would almost certainly survive any such projected divorce, it would not necessarily be a beneficial separation. It would spell the end of a long tradition, and while it is true the dead should never govern the living, things are what they have come out of, and point-to-pointing without the experienced parentage of hunting might make a poor orphan. But at least point-to-pointing has that alternative. For hunting, were the sport to be banned by the European Parliament, there would be no other option but extinction.

So then if hunting does not want to give best to its European opponents, it must do what it was forced to do when it was threatened before. It must pause and take stock of its position in the community, and above all make sure of its support, much of which it might well drum up among the ever-increasing crowds who now go point-to-pointing, always provided that hunting can persuade its more reactionary members to adopt a somewhat more generous and imaginative attitude to its other half, the historic and courageous sport of racing between the flags.

Galloping away into the future, which for the sport looks healthy and bright. Long may it remain so. (John Beasley)

APPENDICES

How It Works

Stewards of Jockey Club (JC)

Point-to-Point Liaison Committee
(to administer and carry out work of point-to-pointing on behalf of JC)
2 members of JC one a JC Steward who is
The Chairman
2 reps from Master of Fox Hounds Association (MFHA)
2 Joint Secs

MFHA Point-to-Point Sub Committee
Chairman
(who is nominated by MFHA not elected)
6/8 MFHA Members*
(to include 1 Draghounds, 1 Harriers, 1 Staghounds reps)
1 member of Point-to-Point Secs Assoc
1 Secretary
1 member of
Point-to-Point Owners' Association (PPOA)**

Point-to-Point Secretaries' Association (PPSA)
(responsible to above sub-com)
consisting of
Reps of all 14 Point-to-Point Areas

* now recommended to be MFHA members with 'hands-on' experience.
** previously and ludicrously (for 9 years!) a non-voting member.

APPENDIX 2

Balance Sheet

Dunham Vale Hunt Point-to-Point Meeting
1989

EXPENDITURE		INCOME	
Schedules	40	Sponsors	1100
Tote Fee	16.50	Adverts	750
Course Rent	1000	Tote	850.59
Insurance	125	Bookies	380
Public Liab.	30	Entries	992
Printing	117	Donations	485.65
Litter Clear.	65	Racecards	3225
Mementoes	125	Car Parks	8735
Floats:		Hunt Club	
Racecards	100	Cars	115
Car Park	500	Cake Stall	254
Hospitality	37.74	Various	115
Formguide	208		
Advert	205		17002.24
PA System	315.53		
Racecards	798		
Red Cross	195.85		
Tents	850.45		
Prize money	945		
Valet	25		
Commentator	83.80		
Car Park Refund	175		
Jockey Club Fee	57.50		
Police	434.24		
Draw Prizes	165.80		
Incidentals	61.96		17002.24
	6677.37		

BALANCE: £10,324.87

(in favour)

Dunham Vale Hunt

Statement of receipts and payments for 1989/90 season General
Account

RECEIPTS	1989/90	PAYMENTS	1989/90
Income from hunting		Masters Guarantee	43000.00
Subs	26885.70	Wire fund	2875.60
Donations	8035.70	Printing, postage,	
Visitors	3270.46	stny, ads.	495.80
Day Money	7274.85	Building Main/nce	5820.39
Car Followers	1653.81	Rates	2975.39
		Buttons/cloth	352.70
	47120.52	Rent	1375.00
		Insurance	1727.89
Contributions		Hon Sec Exps.	1567.00
Buttons/Cloth	488.37		
Point-to-Point		*Donations*	
1988	10324.87	MFHA	285.32
Hunter Trials	750.00	Sec. of Foxhounds	5.00
Spons. Ride	1500.00	BFSS	10.00
Hunt Show	1565.00	BASC	10.00
Ace High Club	1800.00	Show	50.00
Up/Down Ball	315.75	RABI	30.00
Auctions +		Flowers	9.55
Promises +			
Skittles =	3125.90	Bank charges	425.75
League	290.00	Audit fee	325.25
		Misc.	87.45
	20159.89	Vehicles	2987.82
		Farmers Supper	567.80
Building Soc Int	655.78		
	£67936.19		£64983.71
NET SURPLUS	£ 2952.48		

APPENDIX 3

Newspaper Coverage
Form Guides
Results

(*Moderate *****Excellent *****+The Best)

NEWSPAPERS

*The Times***
Brian Beel. Post-meeting, result service, Saturday summary. Occasional race day cover.

*Daily Telegraph****
David Welsh. Best 'daily' coverage. Good articles. Sponsors of championship.

*Independent**
Hugh Condry. Occasional Friday article.

*Sporting Life*****
Michael Williams. Monday results, Wednesday details, Saturday brief forecast. Plenty of photos.

*Racing Post*****
Terry Selby. Results, reports Tuesday. Reports more critical than *Sporting Life*. Criticism usually des- rather than constructive.

*Horse and Hound*****+
Hugh Condry. Full results and reports every Thursday. Plenty of photos (lots now in colour). Ads for and lists of forthcoming meetings. Terrific pre-season cover. The best.

*The Field**
Margaret Reddick. Scant cover, more Hunt interest. List of forthcoming meets. Disappointing.

REVIEWS

*Sporting Life Point-to-Point Results*****
Michael Williams. Review of season past, preview of forthcoming one. Results include comments on placed horses. Statistical record.

*Irish Point-to-Point Results*****
Dan Arnold and Mike Barrett. Lithe Press Co. Comments and ratings horses in training. Invaluable for the serious buyer.

*The Racing Post Record*****+
Mackenzie and Selby's famous or some would have it infamous annual record of point-to-pointers and hunter chasers. Details of everything you need to know, from every horse's form and performances, to the state of the lavatories at Lemalla. Comprehensive coverage and analysis of previous season. Can only really be faulted on its sloppy proof reading, and on its tendency to pronounce. Even so, the point-to-point world would be a duller one without it. The Bible of the sport.

Horses in Training*****
   Published by *Raceform*. What the title says it is.
Timeform*****
   Horses in training with commentary and the best rating service.
   Invaluable guide when back-checking possible purchases from
   professional yards.
Chasers and Hurdlers*****
   Published by *Timeform*. Ratings of every horse which ran under NH
   Rules the previous season, plus comments and pictures.
The Pointer***
   Weekly and annual results publication. Updates during season. 68
   Eagle Brow, Lymm, Cheshire WA13 OU2.
Point-to-Point Index*****+
   Ratings service, cross-referred to *Sporting Life*'s Monday results
   service. 30 Galesbury Rd, Wandsworth, London SW18 2RL 081–870–
   6928.
The Sporting Life National Hunt Results
   Compiled by John Bigby & Colin Havercroft of COSPAC Cambridge.
Programme Book of Steeplechase & Hurdle Races for the season Vol. 2.
   Jan–June.
   Published by Jockey Club, available through Messrs Weatherbys,
   Sanders Rd, Wellingborough, Northants. Essential as it contains full
   list and details of all hunter chases.

APPENDIX 4

Equipment

TACK

Racing Saddle. Make sure leather holders are built into tree and D rings
   for breast girth/plate.
Preferable weight 4 to 6 lb including irons, leathers.
Rawhide leathers.
Racing irons, aluminium, leather, suede grips optional.
Non-elastic girths. Length ranging from 52″ to 60″, usually 54″/56″,
   ¾″ buckles.
Surcingle non-elastic, same width as girth. Ensure long leather part
   with holes to fit variety of size horse.
2 to 3 racing pads usually serge. Gibsons manufacture an excellent one.
Square of lightweight foam for lower weight. Breast plate and breast
   girth elastic. Chamois leather essential.
Weight cloth and lead ¾ stone. Ordinary and lightweight 1½ lb. Spares
   should always be carried in car boot or horse box.

PERSONAL KIT

2 pairs racing breeches.

1 pair waterproofs.

Racing boots, zip and strap at top are best. Others can rub down during race. Good idea to have a spare pair.

Tights – 2 pairs, woollen for cold wet meetings.

Talcum powder for non-zip boots.

Goloshes/plastic bags for muddy conditions. Remember to take off before mounting.

Sweat shirt, polo necked, white/blue. Ski type best.

Silk neckerchief or stock.

Racing colours.

Crash hat.

2 whips.

3 pairs mitts in case of rain.

Racing goggles – 2 pairs.

Elastic bands, variety of sizes, safety pins and aspirin, large flask of tea and a Yorkie!!

Short-sleeved long pullover.

Small towel for cleaning goggles, etc.

Large kit bag.

KIT FOR TRAINING AT HOME

Riding out saddle, leathers, girths, irons, running martingale, sheet for cold mornings.

Racing bridle, large loose ring snaffle, lightweight leather-stitched reins, rubber with at least 12", preferably 16", from end of rubber to buckle makes knotting easier.

Schooling fences, two flights of hurdles and two 3'6" schooling fences.

Area schedules and up-to-date reference books.

RACEDAY KIT

Transport

Travel boots and/or bandages

Tail guard

Knees pads

Travel rug

Head collar

Leading rope

Leather halter

Newmarket chain

Bridle and bit

Reins (unless jockey prefers his or her own)

Irish martingale

Blinkers (if worn)

Paddock sheet

Paddock rug
Sweat sheet
Stable rubbers
Brushing boots
Bandages (if worn)
Strong adhesive tape (to fix boots)
Needle and thread (for sewing bandages on)
Vaseline
Disinfectant
Grooming kit (including needles and plaiting thread)
Gamgee
Cotton wool
Wound powder
Sweat scraper
Sponges
Small water bottle (for washing out horse's mouth prior to race)
Two large water carriers
Two buckets (at least)
Haynet
First aid kit

APPENDIX 5

Some Famous Point-to-Pointers

O'Dell, mostly ridden by his owner Major Harold Rushton to forty victories, including two consecutive Liverpool Fox Hunters.

Pucka Belle, ridden and owned by Mr E. W. Bailey, the winner of 16 races by 1936, culminating with a victory in the National Hunt Chase at Cheltenham.

Duty Paid, winner of 14 of her 19 races run in the years 1936-38.

Halloween, Capt. R. B. Smalley's famous '£90' horse, (which is what he cost initially) and sold on in 1951 in only his second season for £8000 to the Contessa di Sant Elia, whereupon he won 12 steeplechases for her, including the Grand Sefton at Liverpool once and the King George VI at Kempton Twice, as well as running second in the Cheltenham Gold Cup of 1953, and third in the same race for the next three years.

Teal, Mr Ridley Lamb's famous little horse, who won three points in 1951 before going on to win the Grand National the following year, leaving Lord Oaksey (then John Lawrence) of the opinion that he was 'at least the equal of all but a few post-war National winners, and a great deal better than most'.

Four Ten, an immense dark bay Blunderbuss horse, who in 1952 won 4 of his first 6 points, three of them under Percy Tory, before graduating straight to racing under Rules, to go on and win the 1954 Cheltenham Gold Cup.

The Callant, indisputably one of the greatest pointers and hunter chasers of the post-war years, who won 8 points and 3 hunter chases in his first 2 seasons before going on to win the Cheltenham Foxhunters. It is said of Charlie Scott's famous horse that he would have won the Cheltenham Gold Cup of 1957 had he been entered, but his owner would rather hunt him and hack him round the farm. Apparently this amazing horse used to do as many as 25 full days hunting a season, and carried them all, from great to small, the young and the old. He did finally race under Rules, and made a very successful transition, winning 3 good chases in the 1957–8 season, but the owner was said to be happier when the old horse was back on his farm in Jedburgh.

Linwell, the 1957 Cheltenham Gold Cup winner, who also graduated through the ranks of point-to-pointing.

Colledge Master, owned by the extraordinary Mr Lawrence Morgan, who besides piloting his famous horse to all his victories, won an Olympic Gold medal in 1960 in the Three-Day Event, aged 45, bred the winner of the 1947 Australian Derby, and rode Colledge Master to victory in the Liverpool Foxhunters.

Merryman II, a horse sired by the premium hunter stallion Carnival Boy, who won two Ladies' point-to-points before sweeping to victory in the 1959 Liverpool Foxhunters and Scottish Grand National, and the Grand National itself in the following year.

Hard Frost, Mr George Barber's Eastern Counties horse, Hard Frost, winner of 32 Opens, 5 'confined' races, and a hunter chase out of a total of 49 races, run between 1959–64.

Lonesome Boy, the post war record holder with 63 victories, and the longest unbroken sequence (53 wins).

Baulking Green, one of the most amazing hunter chasers ever, owned and bred by Mr Jim Reade, and trained by Captain Tim Forster to win the *Horse and Hound* Cup at Stratford 3 times, and the United Hunts Cup at Cheltenham 4 times, who headed Geoffrey Sales handicap 3 times.

Delilah, the West Country banking pony who between 1954 and 1961 won 48 races.

Corporal Major, a Scottish horse who won 22 out of 44, was only unplaced four times, (winning the Lanarkshire and Renfrewshire Ladies 6 times in succession, and his home Ladies, the Dumfriesshire 6 times out of 7, ridden always by his owner Miss Barbara Paterson.

Puddle Jumper, Guy Cunard's prolific winner of 25 points and three hunter chases out of 66 races.

Mystery Gold, winner of 34 of his 49 races, 31 of them with David Tatlow on board, retired at the age of 16.

Freddie, the most famous of all Scottish horses, and one of the most loved universally, well described as 'the unluckiest horse never to win the Grand National', winner of the then richest prize for hunters, the Vaux National Hunters' Chase at Catterick, the Cheltenham Foxhunters, and when trained under permit by Reg Tweedie in Berwickshire, winner of 8 handicap chases, and runner-up in 2 Grand Nationals to Jay Trump in 1965 and Anglo in 1966.

The Dikler, an incredibly hard-pulling and untypically gigantic son of Vulgan, who in 1969 appeared briefly between the flags, running 4 times, finishing second in his first race, winning his next 2 contemptuously, before playing the rogue and running out in his fourth and last race between the flags under none other than that most accomplished horseman Brian Fanshawe. He was immediately sent to race under Rules where he enjoyed a mighty career under the tutelage of the great Fulke Walwyn.

Spartan Missile, owned and ridden by the late great John Thorne, winner of 23 of his 49 races.

Queensberry Lad, winner of 19 races, whose dam was a gymkhana pony.

Flying Ace, Doreen Calder's great horse, who had won 54 of his 75 races by 1990, including 23 hunter chases.

And most recently:

Border Burg, winner of 13 hunter chases and 17 points by the end of the 1990 season.

Eliogarty, Miss Caroline Beasley's famous chestnut gelding, winner at Cheltenham and Aintree.

Nostradamus, winner of 9 points in 1981.

Tawny Myth, sold by one of the authors when it looked early on as if his career was finished by injury, only for the horse to go on and win 21 of his next 44 races including 3 hunter chases.

Matchplay, the Pidgeon family's magnificent short-running bay gelding, winner of 13 races, including 6 hunter chases.

Sweet Diana, the 'princess of Ladies Opens', the astonishing mare owned by the Dawson family, winner of 24 races between 1985–88, 23 of them being Ladies', and one a hunter chase.

For A Lark, who won all of his ten races in his second season point-to-pointing in 1989, and 5 in 1990.

APPENDIX 6

**Questionnaire to Livery Yard Proprietors
1989**

(The authors are more than grateful to John Dufosee, M. J. Bloom, Charles Sample, Caroline Saunders, John and Jackie Porter and Keith and Janet Cummings, among others, for their invaluable help in contributing the answers to this questionnaire. The answers are NOT given in any particular order, but are chosen at random to try and build up an overall rather than a typical picture. The format also allows for the more knowledgeable reader to take a guess as to who said what . . .)

1. OWNERS

    a. *From what walk of life?*

        Farming, bookmaking, insurance, shipping, property, building, the media, secretarial, computers, wives and widows of above.

        2 farmers, 2 local businessmen, 1 solicitor, 1 owner of marinas, 4 stockbrokers, 1 city analyst, etc.

        3 from London, 1 stockbroker, 1 store manager, 1 director of roofing co., 1 business consultant, 1 director of fabric co., 1 brewer, 1 co. chairman, 1 wine merchant, others are farmers, etc.

        Accountant, farmers, Army, flight charterer, ambulance man, etc.

        As far as I am concerned there is only one livery yard in the whole of the northern area. The majority of the horses are owned, qualified, trained (and ridden) by the same person.

    b. *No. of owner riders.*
        Six
        One
        Six
        Five

    c. *No. of owners requiring jockeys.*
        Ten
        Seven
        Six
        None – all one family

    d. *No. of owners more than 30 miles away.*
        Seven
        Two
        Eight
        All one family

2. HORSES

   a. How many in percentage terms young, unraced, five, six year olds? Homebred or bought in?

     12% last season
     20% untried 5/6 yo.
     50% homebred, 50% bought in
     10–20% varies annually

   b. No. of ex-chasers and hurdlers.

     63%
     Four, one of which had won a novice hurdle
     Three
     n/a

   c. Purchased privately at the sales.

     18%
     Two
     60%/40% several homebred
     n/a

   d. Percentage requiring vet treatment for tendons, etc.

     24%
     Two in five years
     2 horses lost in the season, another struck into (50% chance of recovery), otherwise few problems and none broke down
     15%

3. CHARGES

   a. Basic fee, to include:

     £65 pw to include: general running costs, bedding, feed (not additives), bandages, rugs (small repair charge), everyday medicines (kaolin, Plast, salts, licks, etc.), grooming, clipping, plaiting.

     £80 pw. Includes full livery, gallops, schooling fences, all facilities and transport for hunting (+ plenty of coffee, whisky etc!)

     By arrangement. Includes feeding, exercise, bedding, tack, grooming.

     Private arrangement with owner.

   b. Extras:

     Shoeing: £16.50 per set, £26.50 per set of racing plates. Vet: £150. Kept to minimum, as we use as much of our knowledge as poss. for minor injuries. Costs cover blood tests, X-rays, worming, feed additives.

     Occasional gallop charges, for change of scene for stale horses.

     Entries: £50 on average. (Unless you own Sutton Prince when it's £250.) Hunt Sub: £150 upwards, and sometimes very rarely downwards. Average = £170.

     Shoeing, vet, travel, entries, subs are all usually extras.

     Shoeing, vet, travel, gallops, entries, subs, hire of transport.

c. Transport:

Transport: charged per race. Try not to share for risk of infection. Sometimes necessary.

Transport charged for racing. Shared costs as often send full lorry load.

Own lorry, charge inclusive.

Transport to races charged extra.

Other extras: some yards charge for magnetopulse, postage, etc. Therefore always enquire what extras might not be included *in advance*.

4. WHAT IS YOUR OPINION OF/ATTITUDE TO:

a. Qualifying. How hard do your horses hunt? No. of times for certificate, etc.

Some hunt harder than others. Any with difficult legs or temperament don't hunt so hard, while those that need 'crowd' experience go out more. Average 4/5 outings.

Horses hunted properly for ½ days for 8 days.

Horses are hunted properly and regularly until beginning of January. Green horses might hunt till Feb. They are never taken home tired, because that is when they get hurt. They are taught to jump before they hunt, and they learn their skills properly. Our hunt requires horses to hunt at least 6 times, each horse being issued with a book of tickets, one to be handed out each time it goes out.

Our hunt is an average one, requiring at least 8 days out (½ days).

b. Suggestions for race training.

Horses are individuals, like their owners!

As per individual horse.

They come fit from hunting, and then they have plenty of long slow canters to build them up. Work is conducted over 1½ miles (max), and never at racing pace (unless one gets away!) They then get two or three fast spins to clear out the tubes before racing. They will be schooled as much as is sensible, particularly the young horses, for the more they learn at home the better.

Failing all else, go and listen in the bar of your local N.H. course. All the punters there seem to know!

c. P/P courses. Presentation, fences, going, etc.

Fences need to be standardised. Ground on courses used more than once needs more attention.

Some tracks neglect state of going towards end of season when firming up then becomes dangerous.

Standard of fences must be monitored, and they must be kept big enough. Too many courses (particularly in East Anglia) are

making their fences like hurdles. Courses ideally should be well
drained and level.

Northern courses mainly excellent with well built jumps, which
do not favour horses straight from flat racing or hurdling.

d. *Pet dislikes.*

Grandstand jockeys and trainers!

Ladies riding in Mens' races on unsuitable horses.

New Raceline service. A total waste of time as regards information on going. . . . Bad reports cost both owners and trainers
valuable time and money.

Non triers, human and equine.

Bad losers.

Stewards who do not take a firm hand.

The Jockey Club bureaucracy heaped on volunteer officials at P/P
meetings, and lady riders.

Unfit jockeys.

e. *Feeding.*

Hay, oats, bran, sugar beet, horsehage, additives, but not
necessarily to all the horses.

Hay and nuts with supplements added.

Farm produced oats and hay. Dodson and Horrell feedstuffs,
which if used as instructed need no extra additives. Each horse
has lump of rock salt in their mangers.

Nuts, oats, additives plus hay when needed. Each horse fed to
individual requirements.

Horses fed to their individual needs.

5. <u>FACILITIES</u>

No loose school but access to one 8 furlong straight gallop on
grass. Schooling fences. No all weather.

No loose schooling or all weather facilities. 1½ mile gallop with a
rotavated track alongside, and two large fields for cantering. 4
schooling fences including open ditch. 3 sets of schooling tyres
which are very useful for the youngsters.

Loose school, gallops and fences, but use heath as well. Almost
straight grass gallop plus circular work field and allweather
arena. Can use beach during frost.

Gallops, fences, loose school, plus 40 acre field with straight and
round on hill.

6. <u>GENERAL COMMENTS FOR BEGINNERS:</u>

Newcomers should seek the best advice.

A good book. . .

Point-to-pointing is meant to be fun. Owners should get to know
the staff and team behind the scenes.

Beginners should go to local meetings and look, learn and listen.

Keep a straight line. Think of the horse.

APPENDIX 7

Useful Books

Steeplechasing John Hislop (OOP) (J. A. Allen)*
Point-to-Point Vian Smith (OOP) (Stanley Paul)
Continuing Story of Point-to-Point Michael William (OOP) (Pelham Books)
Introduction to the Thoroughbred Peter Willett (OOP) (Stanley Paul)
The Thoroughbred Peter Willett (Weidenfeld and Nicholson)
Training the Racehorse Lt-Col F. C. Hitchcock (Stanley Paul)
Stable Management and Exercise Capt M. Horace Hayes (OOP) (Stanley Paul)
Horse and Stable Management Jeremy Houghton Brown and Vincent Powell-Smith (BSP Professional Books)
How to Keep Your Horse Healthy Colin Vogel (BSP Books)
Equine Injury and Therapy Mary Bromiley (BSP Books)
Veterinary Notes for Horse Owners Capt M. Horace Hayes (Stanley Paul/ Wyvern Equestrian Books)
Horse Owners Guide to Common Ailments G. W. Serth (OOP) (Pelham Horsemaster Series)
Feeding Your Horse Diana R. Tuke (J. A. Allen)
Getting Your Horse Fit Diana R. Tuke (J. A. Allen)
Getting Horses Fit Sarah Pilliner (BSP Books)
Keeping Horses Susan McBane (BSP Books)
Horse Care Manual Chris May (Stanley Paul)
Black's Veterinary Encyclopedia (A & C Black)
Your First Point to Point Horse Joe Hartigan (OOP) (J. A. Allen)

* OOP signifies out of print. To obtain these try David Jones, Classic Racing Books, 645 St Stephen's Way, Bignall End, Stoke-on-Trent, Staffs. S97 8NL. (0782 722394)

APPENDIX 8

Useful Addresses

ASSOCIATIONS

Point-to-Point Owners' Association (PPOA)

Chairman: T.P. Tory, Crab Farm, Shapwick, Blandford, Dorset DT11 9JL (0258 857206)
President and Chairman of Point-to-Point Committee: J. Mahon, Bishopton Hill House, Stratford-on-Avon, Warwicks (0789 299029)
Secretary: Mrs J. Dawson, Crispins, 90a Ellis Road, Crowthorne, Berkshire RG11 6PN (0344 778438)

Area Representatives

South East W.A. Alcock, The Willows, Brook, Ashford, Kent TN 25 5PD
(Home: 0233 812613; Office: 0233 812761)

Sandhurst C. Coyne, Court Hill, Letcombe Regis, Wantage, Oxon OX12
9JL (02357 2399)

Taunton J.W. Dufosee, Nyland Farm, Gillingham, Dorset SP8 5SG
(0963 70422)

Devon & Cornwall K. Cummings, Eastwood, Bishops Nympton, South
Molton, Devon EX36 4PB (Home: 076 97528; Office: 0823 432356)

West Wales Mrs C. Higgon, Newton Hall, Crundale, Haverfordwest,
Dyfed SA62 4EB (043 782 239)

South Wales Mrs J. Tamplin, Cefn Llwyd Farm, Abertridwr, Caerphilly,
Mid Glamorgan (0222 830278)

Welsh Borders G. Snell, Lower Lulham, Madley, Hereford HR2 9JJ
(Home: 0981 251301; Office: 0981 250253)

West Midlands W. Bush, Old Manor House, West Littleton, Chippenham,
Wilts SN14 8JE (0225 891 683)

South Midlands N. Price, Hill House, Somerton, Oxon OX5 4LR (0869
345210)

East Anglia M. Bloom, Kimberley Home Farm, Wymondham, Norfolk
NR18 0RW (0953 603137)

Midlands The Hon. Mrs R.L. Newton, Church Farm, Saltby, Melton
Mowbray, Leics (0476 860240)

North West T.P. Brookshaw, Lower Vessons, Habberley, Pontesbury,
Shrewsbury, Shropshire (0743 790083)

Yorkshire M.J.R. Bannister M.F.H., Coniston Hall, Coniston Cold,
Skipton, N. Yorkshire (Home: 0756 749551; Office: 0756 748136)

Northern Mrs G. Craigie, Dovecote, Knowesouth, Jedburgh (08356
3642)

Northern Jockeys Representative S. Whittaker, Grange Park Stables, Grange
Park, Wetherby, N. Yorkshire (0937 65122)

Southern Jockeys Representative J.G. Cann, Newland, Cullompton, Devon
EX15 1QQ (0884 32284)

Point-to-Point Secretaries' Association (PPSA) See Appendix 9.

Jockey's Association
Bridge St, Newbury (0635 44102)

JOCKEY'S EQUIPMENT

Stockists
Gibsons, Newmarket.
Wick's, Lambourn.
Giddings, Bond St. London.
Jockey's Assoc. Newbury (for all equipment).

(Also good local network of dealers who generally advertise in *Horse and
Hound*.)

APPENDIX 9

List of Area Secretaries

Point-to-Point Secretaries Association

Chairman: Mrs C. Higgon, Newton Hall, Crundale, Haverfordwest, Pembrokeshire SA62 4EB (043 782 239)

Vice-Chairman: W.H. Batten, Esq., Church House, Yeovil, Somerset (0935 23685)

Secretary: John Hickman, Esq., 11 Grosvenor Crescent, London SW1X 7EE (071 245 6521)

Addresses for Area Schedules

Each Schedule gives full details of every meeting and race planned for 1990 in each Area. They may be obtained by sending a stamped SAE (at least 9″ by 6″) to the following:

South East (Kent, Sussex & Surrey): J.C.S. Hickman, Esq., Romney House, Ashford Market, Elwick Road, Ashford, Kent TN23 1PG (Home: 0233 72397; Office: 0233 622222)

Sandhurst (Surrey, Hampshire & Isle of Wight): M.T. Ward, Esq., Wokefield Park, Stratford Mortimer, nr. Reading, Berks (0734 222504)

Taunton (Somerset, Dorset, Wilts): F.G. Matthews, Esq., Peak Ashes, Chattle Lane, Penselwood, Wincanton, Somerset BA9 8LY (0747 840412)

Devon & Cornwall: P. Wakeham, Esq., Torne House, Rattery, South Brent, Devon (03644 3252)

West Wales: Mrs C. Higgon, Newton Hall, Crundale, Haverfordwest, Pembrokeshire SA62 4EB (043 782 239)

South Wales & Monmouthshire: P.H. Curry, Esq., South Cottage, Penmark, Barry, S. Glamorgan (Home: 0446 710436; Office: 0222 627587)

Welsh Border Counties: J.R. Pike, Esq., The Priory, Kilpeck, Hereford (098 121 366)

West Midlands (Gloucestershire, Worcestershire & Warwickshire): A.N. Champion, Esq., 1 Foregate St, Worcester WR1 1DB (Home: 029 921 416; Office: 0905 28366)

South Midlands (Warwickshire, Oxon, Berks, Bucks): Col. A. Clerke-Brown, OBE, Kingston Grove, Kingston Blount, Oxon OX9 4SQ (0844 51356)

East Anglia: A.J. Round, Esq., Roundbush Farm, Layer Marney, Colchester, Essex CO5 9XB (0206 330239)

Midlands (Lincolnshire, Northants & Notts): The Hon. Mrs R.L. Newton, Church Farm, Saltby, Melton Mowbray, Leics (0476 860240)

North West (Shropshire, Cheshire): J. Wilson, Esq., Huntington House, Little Wenlock, Telford, Salop TF6 5BW (0952 502354)

Yorkshire: Miss C.M. Bolitho, Low Carr, Ampleforth, Yorkshire TO6 4ED (Home: 03476 600; Office: 04393 77)

Northern (Northumberland, Scotland): C.J. Sample, ARICS, Estate Office, Bothal Castle, Morpeth, Northumberland (0670 513128)

APPENDIX 10

Selected Livery Yards

John & Jackie Porter, Hampstead Holt Farm, Kintbury, Berks RG15 0DD (0488 58346)

Geoff Coatsworth, Mill House, Meldon, Morpeth, Northumberland

Michael & Jenny Bloom, Kimberley Home Farm, Wymondham, Norfolk

Caroline Saunders, Holderby North Lodge, Spratton, Northampton NN6 8LG (0604 770423)

John & Jane Dufosee, Nyland Farm, Gillingham, Dorset (0963 70422)

Keith & Janet Cummings, Eastwood, Bishop's Nympton, Devon (07697 528)

Paul Hacking, Pelsham Farm, Peasmarsh, Rye, East Sussex (0797 21206)

Dick & Joyce Bainbridge, Upper Hill Farm, Hill, Berkeley, Glos GL13 9EE (0454 260 229)

Robert & Sally Alner, Locketts Farm, Droop, Struminster, Newton, Dorset DT11 0EZ (0258 817271)

Robert & Teresa Elwell, Copredy Barn, Copredy, Banbury, Oxon (029575 750)

Caroline Gordon c/o Mrs G. Knight, Lockinge Manor, Wantage, Oxon (0235 831968)

Mike & Tim Stephenson, The Smithy, Castle Morton, Malvern, Worcs (0684 813 12)

Stephen Brookshaw, Preston Farm, Uffington, Shrewsbury, Salop

David Smith, Kirby Ridge Farm, Stokesley, North Yorks

APPENDIX 11

Leading Post-War Point-to-Point Riders

In order of total winning rides:

D Turner*	343	R Davies	97
Maj G Cunard	268	R Hunt	97
J Llewellyn*	230	P Hamer*	96
F Ryall	218	T S Jeanes	95
G Cann	217	Mrs L Gibbon	93
R Miller	178	D Gibson	91
J Daniell	175	F Mathias	91
Mrs J Sheppard	173	T Holland-Martin	89
Mrs P Tollit	171	R Treloggen*	88
R Hacking	170	I McKie*	87
M Felton*	166	R Chugg	84
P Greenall	160	N Bush*	82

R Alner*	152	W Elliot	82
J Sharp*	146	Miss P Fisher*	82
M Bloom	145	R Shepherd	82
Mrs S Horton	145	A Charlton	80
A E Hill	136	Mrs D Chown	80
R Guilding	135	S Crank*	80
T Rooney*	134	J Dufosee	79
D Tatlow	133	P Scouller*	79
Miss J Pigeon	126	M Arthers*	78
M Williams (Wales)	124	A Berry	78
S Brookshaw*	119	R Bloomfield	78
Mrs S French*	119	H Cowell	77
J Bryan	115	G Cooper*	76
Miss A Dare*	115	J Frost	76
C Down*	115	P Craggs*	75
P Scholfield*	114	J Docker	75
W Jones	113	R Cowell	74
D Wales	110	Mrs M Crouch	74
T Wilkin	109	T Philby	74
R Greenway	108	A Ulyet*	74
J Newton*	107	T Jones*	73
Col C Spencer	107	Mrs J Dawson*	72
M Williams (Devon)	103	Miss S Morgan*	72
C Macmillan	101	P Warren	71
R Edwards	100	W Foulkes	70
R Woolley	99	D Kinsella*	70
G Barber	97	H Rowe	70

* still race-riding

APPENDIX 12

Champion Point-to-Point Riders

	Gentlemen			Ladies	
1946	A Grantham	6	1946	Miss I Coxon	4
	H May	6		Miss K Tatham-Warter	4
	T Southern	6	1947	Miss A Covell	5
	R Turner	6		Miss M Coke	5
1947	W How	14	1948	Miss K Tatham-Warter	4
1948	Maj P Rawlings	11		Miss J Brutton	4
1949	Maj G Cunard	20	1949	Miss K Tatham-Warter	7
1950	A Hill	19	1950	Miss D Brooke	8
1951	Maj G Cunard	12	1951	Miss P Rushton	9

Year	Name		Year	Name	
1952	Maj G Cunard	15	1952	Miss G Moore	8
1953	Maj G Cunard	13	1953	Miss G Moore	9
1954	F Ryall	13	1954	Miss J Renfree	7
	J Trevisick	13	1955	Miss J Renfree	13
1955	J Everitt	15	1956	Miss J Renfree	11
1956	E Greenway	12	1957	Mrs S French	8
	F Mathias	12		Miss J Renfree	8
1957	Maj R Ingall	14	1958	Miss D Guilding	8
1958	R Edwards	12		Miss J Renfree	8
	N Williams	12	1959	Mrs D Coaker (née Brooke)	12
1959	D Wales	16	1960	Mrs P Tollit (née Rushton)	9
1960	R Edwards	14	1961	Miss F Robarts	10
	F Ryall	14	1962	Mrs P Tollit (Née Rushton)	9
1961	J Daniell	16	1963	Miss S Rimell*	5
1962	A E Hill	12	1964	Mrs P Tollit (née Rushton	10
1963	Maj G Cunard	15	1965	Mrs P Tollit (née Rushton)	15
1964	Maj G Cunard	22	1966	Miss U Brander-Dunbar	10
1965	D Tatlow	18	1967	Mrs P Hinch	11
1966	D Tatlow	25	1968	Miss S Aston	15
1967	D Tatlow	24	1969	Miss J Turner	14
1968	D Tatlow	18	1970	Miss S Aston	14
1969	M Bloom	19	1971	Miss S Aston	14
1970	D Turner	19	1972	Miss S Aston	15
1971	R Davies	29		Mrs P Tollit (née Rushton)	15
1972	R Miller	21	1973	Mrs M Forrest	17
1973	R Miller	23	1974	Mrs J Bothway (née Turner)	20
1974	D Turner	26	1975	Mrs J Bothway (née Turner)	17
1975	D Turner	24	1976	Mrs J Bothway (née Turner)	17
1976	D Turner	22	1977	Mrs J Shepherd (née Turner)	17
1977	D Turner	29	1978	Mrs R White	11
1978	J Bryan	32	1979	Miss P Fisher	10
1979	D Turner	17	1980	Miss L King	14
1980	I McKie	20	1981	Miss L King	14
	D Turner	20	1982	Miss J Pigeon	18
1981	I McKie	18	1983	Miss J Pigeon	18
1982	P Greenall	24	1984	Miss M Lingard	13
1983	J Llewellyn	19		Miss J Pigeon	13
1984	D Turner	20**	1985	Miss J Pigeon	18
	P Greenall	19	1986	Miss A Dare	19
1985	P Greenall	23	1987	Miss A Dare	17
1986	P Greenall	28	1988	Mrs J Litston	16
1987	M Felton	26	1989	Miss L Crow	15
1988	P Scholfield	37	1990	Miss A Dare	20
1989	M Felton	26			
1990	M Felton	27			

* 11 Ladies each had 5 winners – Miss Rimell had the most 2nds
** included 2 walk-overs (one by prior arrangement)

GLOSSARY

Auntie, waving to (*See also* Cab, hailing a) When the jockey sticks one arm out for balance when a horse catches him/her out over a jump.

Baby As in 'a bit of a'. Means the horse is either faint hearted or needs more time, usually six or seven more years.

Bleeder Various connotations, usually a horse which bbvs (breaks blood vessels). Generally not at all detectable in pre-purchase examinations, unless horse's lungs are extensively damaged, and will rarely, if ever, be revealed in pre-purchase gallop as horse will not be match fit, therefore always suspect likely looking horses for sale from posh yards. If the horse is sound everywhere else, why then is it being sold? No drugs allowed by JC to control this most wretched of conditions, with the exception of the homoeopathic paste and powder X-bleed now on sale and widely used.

Blinder Not as in the night before the morning after, but as in 'didn't he/she run a blinder' – a horse that ran, as they say on Channel 4, a Big Race.

Blinds Blinkers, visors (qv). Used, it is said, to help make the horse concentrate on the job. Said to be at their most effective first time on.

Bold Used either honestly to describe a horse's brave style of jumping, or euphemistically when trying to get someone to ride a lunatic, as in 'he's nice and bold' . . .

Bone As in 'plenty of', 'eight inches of', etc. Horses are said to need plenty of bone to race, the minimum requirement being 8″. It is conveniently forgotten when boasting of a horse's 'bone' that to measure the cannon bone the tape has to go right round the leg, including tendons *et al*. The most sensible way to look at 'bone' in the cannon is short and straight and strong. 9″ bone with big tendons is no better nor no worse than 7″ of good straight bone without such fat attachments behind. A case for the experts when buying.

Bullfinch A type of fence no longer met point-to-pointing. Formerly a normal hedge with a 'screen' of birch above, through which you had to jump.

Cab, hailing a See Auntie, waving to.

Chemist The vet.

Cough Usually a sign of the dreaded virus. Sometimes horses cough early in the day due to dusty bedding, but a cough usually heralds trouble, particularly after work.

Courses Horses for. There is truth in the saying, and certain horses go better on some courses than others, either because they prefer left to right handed or vice versa, or because they need or don't need a 'distance' (qv). Some tracks ride 'long', others 'short'. (See text.)

Cudgel The whip. *See* pp. 123–127.

Cutting Down One of the many excuses offered for the sale of a horse. Professional trainers or big owners said to be 'cutting down' are more generally weeding out the useless horses.

Distance A horse said to 'need the distance' usually means in trainer-speak that he's a plodder and needs a track where stamina counts. *See* Courses, also see track details in Mackenzie and Selby.

DIY Doing It Yourself. Training the hard way but also the most rewarding way.

Dog An ungenuine horse.

Easily As in 'won easily' or 'as he liked' or more recently 'won doing handsprings'. Either all the others fell or were 'having an easy' (qv), or the horse is genuinely exceptional and should be followed until beaten. In point-to-pointing, the form line is much more dependable than under Rules and should be respected.

Easy As in 'given an easy'. A schooling ride (qv), strictly against the rules but a common occurrence, to say the least. Sometimes called 'an introduction'. *Sporting Life* made a valiant attempt in 1990 to attract the attention of the stewards to this practice by publishing a list of runners who had finished p.u. (pulled up) on their first run, only to win next time out. It made no difference.

Enquiry A convening of the stewards whereby they meet to see if any of them noticed what was going on, and if so, whether or not they should do anything about it. Not to be confused with Enquiry, Stewards', as in National Hunt or Flat Racing, which is a different sort of affair altogether. An endangered species, and almost extinct in Wales.

Entire A horse with a different sort of 'everything' (qv). A stallion, and a very rare sight on the point-to-pointing course.

Entries One of the most important parts of the game. Knowing where and when to enter is an art form in itself. (See text.)

Everything As in 'he's got everything on him bar the kitchen sink'. The horse is a puller or bolter and is wearing every device known to the trainer to control him.

Farrier With your vet, the most important member of the racing yard. If he is good at his job, he will invariably be rude, or else will be married to a woman who is rude, but all this must be tolerated, because as the adage has it, no farrier – no horse.

Fencing The racing verb for 'jumping', as in 'the horse has been sent fencing'. Has nothing to do with fencing as in sword play, or post and rail.

Fired A neolithic and barbaric way of treating lameness, done by the application of a red hot iron to the horse's skin. To quote Captain Hayes FRCVS, 'there is no scientific evidence to support its use, and the author considers it valueless and an unnecessary mutilation of the horse'. Enough said.

Friendless As in 'friendless in the market'. Not being backed seriously, if at all, and therefore the horse is probably out for an 'easy' (qv).

Front Runner Either a horse which cannot be held up, or more generally a horse whose best hope of winning is to lead from the start and hope everyone else falls.

Gallops In point-to-point terms, the side of a friendly farmer's field, a bit of hill, a stretch of common land, anywhere the horses can have a bit of fast work.

Give As in ground, meaning on the soft side, or as in horse, such as 'he doesn't give', meaning he (she or it) is a non-trier.

Going A set of euphemisms to describe the state of the ground. Hard = Concrete. Firm/Hard = Concrete. Firm = Very Hard. Good to Firm = Hard. Good = Firm, or Firm to Hard. Good to Soft = On the Good side of Firm. Soft = Good. Very Soft = Yielding. Yielding = Heavy. Heavy = Unbelievable. Very Heavy = Unraceable.

Grackle Not to be confused with grockle (qv). A type of noseband meant to help in the control of strong pullers.

Grockle Not to be confused with above. A derogatory term meant to have originated in the West Country to describe holiday visitors. The non-cognoscenti as far as racing goes, and easily identified as the punters backing any horses at a price longer than 10/1. The bookmakers' friend.

Ground As in 'needs the ground'. Trainerspeak for saying your horse needs the mud, not for himself, but to slow up his opponents. Can therefore be taken to mean your horse is not very quick.

Half-lengthing The technique of taking off at the same time as a horse which is half a length up on you, hoping to force an error. *See* p. 170.

Held Up Usually coupled with 'produced'. Instructions to the pilot would be 'hold him up and produce him two from home'. Often easier said than done.

Hold A horse that has 'taken hold' can be said to have taken charge. 'He likes to take hold' means you the jockey won't stand a chance of controlling him.

Humpty As in 'went humpty at the last', meaning to fall.

Ideal Ride Horses for sale are often described as an 'ideal ride' for an amateur, or a lady, or a novice. It can generally be taken to mean the horse is safe but slow in terms of a novice ride, or small in the instance of a lady's ride.

Idling Usually done from the front. A horse will often 'idle' when left in front too early with nothing to race against. Jockeys sometimes idle, but not for the same reasons.

Indian File A procession. Not the best sort of race.

Jammy Lucky. As in lying a distant second when the favourite runs out at the last.

Jockette A female pilot (qv).

Kitchen Sink See Everything.

Ladies' Ride A small fast horse.

Leg, done a Broken down. More often than not the damage will have been done to a tendon, and will require immediate attention and rest. (*See* Firing.)

Likes To Be Often part of a jockey's instructions, as in 'the horse likes to be settled/up front/tailed off/covered up/given his head,' etc, as if the horse had any say in the matter.

Livery Yards The acceptable definition of a training yard, in the Jockey Club's mind there being no such thing as.

Makes a Noise A horse which has usually gone in the wind (qv) is said to roar, or make a noise. Can also be applied to certain owners, although not in reference to their wind.

Mares Female stallions, allowed 5lb.

Needs Trainerspeak for what the horse is not yet doing. As in 'needs further/shorter/softer/harder,' etc.

Nose, got a All horses have noses, but to have a nose means to have a runny nose, which in turn is a sign of something wrong.

Noseband X Seen in the reference books. 'So and So runs in a X noseband.' A sure sign of a 'puller' (qv).

Off, to be Very confusing. Means in betting terms that the horse is fancied by connections and will be expected to go close. Cynics take it to mean that on this particular occasion when the horse is 'off' it will be really trying.

Open Ditch A trench in front of a hedge, of varying depth. All courses must have one.

Orders A set of instructions given to the jockey by the trainer in private, not in front of the owner. The real tactics for a race are worked out in advance, and the last thing the trainer wants is the owner coming in with his tuppenceworth. The trainer will in this instance know best, because he has probably overheard some other trainers' instructions, and/or knows which horses are 'off' (qv).

Owners A happy band of folk who by and large are blissful in their ignorance, but love the sport. However, enthusiastic owners who give detailed orders (qv) as the jockey is trying to mount a bucking and plunging half ton of thoroughbred should best be ignored.

Owner-trainers A different breed from the above; often members of families with a long tradition in the sport, usually racing home-bred and home-trained horses.

Pace As in 'off the pace', meaning the horse is going so slowly and is so far behind that it is without a chance bar a major debacle.

Passport All racehorses must have a passport, issued by Weatherbys, and which must be 'up to date', viz. the animal's vaccinations must be current. If not, and any anomaly is discovered, the horse may not run, or may be disqualified retrospectively.

Pilot Jockey.

PPOA The Association of Point-to-Point Owners, a worthy body whose influence over the sport is happily increasing (*see* Appendix 8).

Produced See Held Up.

Pulled Up A horse is deemed to have pulled up when when the rider considers he has no chance and runs the horse out at a fence and pulls it up. Not always a reliable form guide however (*see* Easy).

Puller See Hold and Noseband X.

Quiet Ride Useless.

Rasper A stiff fence out hunting.

Reluctant to Start Doesn't like racing and will not start unless a bomb goes off behind it.

Roars See Makes a Noise.

Rogue A bad tempered and useless beast, the sort of ride jockeys get offered on the course.

Run Off As in feet. Trainerspeak. ' 'Fraid he was run off his feet' means your horse is a plug.

Sales Held most successfully at Doncaster and Ascot as far as point-to-pointing is concerned. Some remarkable bargains can be found at the sales, but expert guidance is needed. (See text.)

Schooling Teaching a horse to jump at home. Also done in public during a race, although illegal. Very hard to spot and punish when done skilfully, and an 'accepted' illegality since owing to a shortage of home gallops, few horses are produced fit first time out.

Slipped Up A horse which fell over when not jumping anything.

Spun A horse rejected as 'unsound' by the vet after examination.

Start The beginning of a race, and often the most controversial part.

Stewards Adult school prefects. Their National Hunt counterparts were once famously described by John Francome as 'cabbage patch dolls', which takes a bit of topping. Often ex-Army Majors, and anyone who has served in the Army will need no further definition. There are certainly some exceptionally good and intelligent stewards, but as always, the exception proves the rule.

Thruster A style of riding born in the hunting field whereby certain horsemen will force their way past mid-jump. On the racecourse this sort of rider will try to 'come up the inside', which is not on, unless the horse being overtaken is beaten. Men have killed for less.

Tongue Straps A device to stop a horse 'swallowing' its tongue, a habit some horses have which doesn't help their breathing.

Trainerspeak Professional lingo (see above). In most cases the best way of understanding it is to substitute the word 'money' for 'time'. Thus in 'your horse needs time' this can be taken to mean it is going to cost you money in training fees before it ever sees the racecourse. 'As long as you're patient, if you've got the time' = if you can afford it, etc.

Tubed Or 'hobdayed'. An operation to help a horse which has 'broken wind' or any other serious respiratory troubles. Used to be done by cutting a hole in the horse's neck, and sticking a plug in it, which was removed for racing. Today the operation can be done in other ways, either by tying back the paralysed side of the larynx or simply by inserting a tube in the trachea and thus bypassing the obstruction. Horses very often win first time out after being hobdayed.

Unseated Polite parlance for the jockey falling off after the horse has jumped and not fallen.

Up the Inside See Thruster. Guy Cunard's least favourite type of person was an 'up-the-insider'.

Useless Not a very good horse.

Vet Someone who earns every crate of Scotch you must send him at Christmas.

Virus The bane of horse training. Some theorists attribute the prevalence of equine flu and the 'virus' to the animals' immunity system having been weakened by compulsory vaccination.

Visor A form of blinker, with holes cut in the sides enabling the horse to have some sight of his opponents. Said to be a sign of an ungenuine horse. Horses wearing them, or blinkers, often win first time out, after which their effectiveness wears off.

Walk-Over A one horse race, whereby the only contestant is simply required to gallop past the judges' box to notch up another victory. It is mooted that in future walk-overs shall not count in the championship contests.

Water Jump Not compulsory, but still to be found on occasional courses.

Wind, gone in the See Tubed, Roars, Makes a Noise. A horse which has gone in the wind is usually suffering from laryngeal hemiplegia, in which case the left-hand side of the larynx is completely or partially paralysed. Most can be treated surgically, although the horse's performance generally suffers as a result.

X Bred The sort of part bred horse who used to race point-to-point, but is now only to be seen occasionally in Members' Races.

X-cuses Trainerspeak. Reasons given to the owner for the failure of his horse. A good trainer and a good jockey will always have a good store of tactful excuses so that the owner need not be unduly discouraged. To all owners, geese are swans.

Yuppie The young who go racing in Oxford, Berkshire, and some parts of Wiltshire.

Zed What point-to-point trainers do in the summer.

INDEX

Figures in italics refer to illustrations